French Wines
Ordinary and Extraordinary
(Vins ordinaires et extraordinaires)

by

VIVIAN ROWE

HARRAP   LONDON

First published in Great Britain 1972

by **GEORGE G. HARRAP & CO. LTD**

182-184 High Holborn, London WC1V 7AX

© *Vivian Rowe* 1972

ISBN 0 245 50833 3

*Composed in IBM Press Roman type and printed
by Redwood Press Limited, Trowbridge, Wiltshire*

Made in Great Britain

CONTENTS

Introduction

This is a factual book on the lesser rather than the greater wines of France. Many excellent books on the greater rather than the lesser ones already exist, but this little book has something rather different to offer.

Its principal emphasis is on the great number of enjoyable French wines of medium quality sold at prices within the means of a majority of wine-drinkers, including young people just developing a taste for wine. In the comprehensive index they can look up the name of a wine and at least learn what part of France it comes from and what kind of a wine it is. Any French wine not sold under a commercial brand name and which a wine merchant is likely to be offering is virtually certain to be described, however briefly.

It lays hardly less emphasis on the needs of the motorist travelling through France who, all too often, through lack of knowledge of what to look for and ask for in the wine-rich provinces, fails to make his journey the inexpensive voyage of wine-discovery or the personal itinerant wine-tasting it could have been.

The wine index refers the reader to some 450 different French wines, each one of which is located geographically and briefly summed up. Five suggested routes, all starting in the North, between them cover virtually all that part of France in which vineyards flourish. This vast area amounts to some seven-eighths of the whole country. Four areas which seemed too important – and in two cases too complicated – to fit into a road pattern are the subject of four separate, compact chapters: these are Alsace, Champagne, Bordeaux, and Burgundy.

The 450 wines are divided into three categories. First, to the number of 300, come those regulated by an *appellation contrôlée (A.C.)*, which means they are submitted to very strict control over place of origin, types of grape, number of vines per hectare, alcohol and sugar content, and in some cases even further details when these might influence the quality of the wine. All the finest French wines come under an *appellation contrôlée*, but not all *appellation contrôlée* wines are necessarily of top grade and price. On the contrary, the majority of them are sound and reliable wines providing pleasant drinking at reasonable cost.

The second category, amounting to some fifty wines, includes those entitled to be sold as *vins délimités de qualité supérieure (V.D.Q.S.)*. The degree of control over these is far less wide than for *A.C.* wines and is chiefly concerned with the careful delimitation of the area within which the wines bearing its name may be produced. This is a comparatively recent introduction, at least in terms of the slowly changing wine trade, but it has already proved to be a useful factor in the raising of standards in what were previously categories of wines of very inconstant quality.

Finally we come to the little *vins de pays (V.P.)*, local wines bearing the name of an area but submitted to very little control. The semi-official *La Protection des Appellations d'Origine* says of them that "they are all *vins ordinaires* whose quality is highly variable . . ." About 100 of them are named in this book and included along one or other of the five routes, and they must all be accepted as conforming to this description. The author has tasted most of them, but some are recommendations from friends. They are sometimes on the rough side and occasionally a little earthy, but they are all cheap and if you should not happen to like them at least the experience will not have been an expensive one. It is also true that every now and then, when the weather happens to have been particularly favourable right up to the vintage, one or two will be so much better than you had any right to expect that you will have a delightful surprise and be flushed by the warming feeling of successful discovery.

This is a very personal book. Over the years the author has had exceptional opportunities for tasting wine over a very wide area of France. It has usually been wine for people of modest means rather than magnificent vintage wine, and he has enjoyed the experience. He is not connected with the wine trade and claims no knowledge beyond what has come to him within this journeying. His judgment is therefore personal, reflecting his own likes and dislikes, and he expects readers often to disagree with it. Other writers on wine matters certainly will.

It should not be forgotten that this was conceived as a practical book for, lacking professional experience, it would be ridiculous for him to pontificate. He also lacks that refinement of the senses which enables experts, for example, to discern in a wine "a just perceptible smokiness at the back of its floweriness"; it is therefore a book of simple statement.

Comments by readers and details of any wines they have met which are not in this book will always be welcome.

Wine and Wine Words

WINE

According to encyclopedia and dictionary, "wine is the fermented juice of the grape". It is a very complex liquid. At the beginning of the wine-making process, when the grapes are squeezed, a viscid fluid flows out of them. This juice is, technically, the 'must'. It is particularly liable to spontaneous fermentation when exposed to the heat of the sun, due to minute specks of yeast which cling to the skin. Either as microscopic particles in suspension or in solution in the water content, the must holds two kinds of sugar (laevulose and dextrose), pectin, gums, dextrin, gluten, tartaric acid, potassium, racemic and malic acids, and such odd items as silicon, iron, and manganese in the form of oxides, some potassium sulphate and calcium phosphate, as well as common salt. A laboratory synthesis of this complicated natural product seems, therefore, to be a very remote possibility.

Even when the fermentation caused by the yeast has come to an end, water is still the major constituent of the fermented must, but it now holds — again, either in suspension or solution — various alcohols and ethers, as well as tannic and other acids, and glycerine.

All grapes when pressed give a yellowish juice. White wines can come equally well from purple or from white grapes. Red wines are made from purple grapes and derive their colour from the skins during fermentation. The best white wines are given only a very light pressing to ensure a limpid, pleasing colour in the resultant wine. Most Champagne is made from purple grapes and great care has to be taken to avoid contact with the lightly pressed, barely punctured skin.

What still remains mysterious is the way in which different soils give quite dissimilar flavour to wines made from similar grapes. The famous white Graves of Bordeaux are made from Sémillon, Sauvignon, and Muscadelle grapes. So are the white wines of Gaillac where these same grapes grow on the banks of the river Tarn, on the very edge of the Massif Central. Yet nobody could possibly confuse the two wines.

After variety of grape and variety of soil, the third great influence to which wine is submitted is sunshine. In the long run, it is the amount of sunshine at the right time which determines the sugar content of the must. It also has an important bearing on the fullness of flavour. The alcoholic content of the wine is basically determined by the amount of sugar in the must. The sun is a major factor in creating the sugar content which, converted into alcohol by fermentation, gives the wine (in very general terms) the degree of alcohol needed to improve with age and travel well.

SOME WINE WORDS WHICH OCCUR IN THIS BOOK

Alcohol
The alcoholic strength of wines is indicated throughout by the French system (Gay-Lussac), which indicates the percentage of alcohol in the liquid by volume. By this system, the British *proof spirit* would be rated at 57.10⁰.

Aligoté
The name of a grape used in the preparation of dry white wines. Bourgogne-aligoté is much favoured as a basis for *vin blanc cassis* (also known as *Kir*).

Appellation contrôlée
See the description in the Introduction.

Botrytis cinerea
Also known as "noble rot". See the description in Route III, in connection with the wines of Monbazillac.

Cassis
Blackcurrant cordial with an alcoholic content of some

30°, mostly made in Dijon and in universal use as an addition to dry white wine to make the inexpensive aperitif known as *Vin blanc cassis* or *Kir.* It has no connection with Cassis on the Mediterranean coast or the wine which takes its name.

Clairet
A red wine of particularly limpid colour.

Clairette
A wine made from the white grape of this name.

Climat
A word used in Burgundy in the same sense as the word *cru* is used in the Bordeaux area (see *Cru* below).

Crémant
Describes a sparkling wine with a less vigorous sparkle than a *mousseux.*

Cru
No single English word will describe all the shades of meaning *cru* has in French. Basically it means a plot of land in agricultural use, and by extension is most often applied to a vineyard or group of vineyards in close proximity, and to the product of the vineyard or vineyards. In English it is usually referred to as a *growth* and is in constant use in connection with the wines of Bordeaux. In Burgundy, the *cru* becomes a *climat* when referring to a vineyard.

Edelzwicker
In Alsace, a blend of wines made from "noble" grapes.

Gewürztraminer
High-quality Alsatian wine; the best is made from very late-gathered grapes.

Graves
White and red Bordeaux wines grown on gravel slopes.

Gros-plant
The name of a rather coarse grape from which a dry white wine is made round the estuary of the river Loire.

Kir
Alternative name for *vin blanc cassis* (see *Cassis*, above), from Canon Kir, courageous Mayor of Lyons under the German occupation, whose favourite drink it was.

Mousseux
Describes a fully sparkling wine.

Muscat
Sweet white wines made entirely or mainly from the muscat grape, which gives them a rich muscatel flavour.

Must
The juice pressed out of grapes.

Nature
Description applied to a still version of a wine better known as a sparkling one – for example, *Champagne* and *Champagne nature.*

Passe-tout-grains
A red Burgundy made from a mixture mainly of Pinot and Gamay grapes, and a smaller proportion of Chardonnay.

Pelure-d'Oignon
A red wine of the Jura, developing a light tawny colour, from which it takes this colloquial name of "onion skin".

Pétillant
Describes a wine in which air bubbles rise slowly and infrequently as compared with a *mousseux.*

Picpoul (or Piquepoult) de Pinet
Name of a variety of grape from which a Languedoc white wine is made.

Pinot-Chardonnay
A white Burgundy from Mâcon, made from these high-quality grapes.

Rancio
Sweet white wines from Banyuls, Côtes-d'Agly, Côtes-de-Haut-Roussillon, Maury, or Rivesaltes which have been allowed to age and mellow beyond the ordinary, and which in consequence develop a particular tawny colour and an intensified flavour and sweetness.

Rosé-de-Cabernet
Rosé wines from the Loire made from the high-grade Cabernet grape.

Roussette, Rousselet
White wines made from the Roussette grape.

Schillerwein, or *Clairet-d'Alsace*
An Alsatian red wine of particularly clear colour.

Traminer
An Alsatian wine made from the grape of the same name, which has not been allowed to become overripe as with the *Gewürztraminer.*

Vin blanc
White wine.

Vin délimité de qualité supérieure (V.D.Q.S.)
A lower-grade "certificate of merit" than the *appellation contrôlée (A.C.)* accorded to secondary wines from certain well-defined areas.

Vin de liqueur
Sweet dessert wine fortified with not less than 15 per cent of 90° alcohol.

Vin de paille
Wine made in the mountains of the east of France and in

the Hermitage area of the Rhone valley, usually in
February or March, from late-gathered grapes which have
been maturing on beds of straw since the grape harvest.

Vin de sable
White wine of a very light colour made from grapes
growing in sandy soil.

Vin doux naturel
One would expect a "natural sweet wine" to be an unfort-
ified one. In fact it is a naturally sweet wine fortified with
not less than 5 per cent and not more than 15 per cent of
90° alcohol.

Vin gris
A *vin de pays* to be found in Eastern France and in
Auvergne made from the simultaneous pressing of approximately equal quantities of black grapes and white grapes,
which produces a juice of indeterminate colour almost
justifying the description "grey". It makes a change from
the ordinary run of local reds and whites, but is never a
wine of any distinction.

Vin de pays (V.P.)
Local wines without pretension labelled with the name of
a particular area, mostly perfectly good for low-cost
drinking but not of any refinement.

Vin jaune
White wine of a very deep colour, made from late-gathered
grapes.

Vin ordinaire
A wine without distinction intended for daily consumption
at a minimum cost. It carries no guarantee of any kind. It
may well be a blend, which can include wines brought in
from outside France, or a stark wine from the Languedoc
area or from any other nameless vineyard. The buyer is
entirely dependent upon the honesty of the vendor as to
whether or not he gets value for his money. It says much

for the French that their *vins ordinaires* are so often quite
palatable, even though lacking in individual flavour.

Vin rosé
A light red wine, made in many parts of France, usually
from black grapes; the lighter colour is obtained by either
using only a small proportion of the skins, or by leaving
the skins in contact with the wine for a very short period.
Pink champagne is coloured with a little addition of a
red wine of the area, and a similar process is used in some
other areas. There are suspicions that colorants not de-
rived from the grape are used in some districts to overcome
the problem of colour fading.

Vin rouge
Red wine.

Zwicker
Alsatian blended wines of a lower quality than the
Edelzwicker (see above).

Vines and Vineyards

The vine is a very ancient plant, and *Vitis vinifera* has been developed by the ingenuity of man from dates so remote that there is no definite record of them, but grape pips have been found in Europe in Bronze Age graves. The use of the grape for producing alcohol by natural means goes back to the beginning of man's recorded history.

Records of French vineyards of reasonable credibility go back to the Roman occupation, but it is believed that the Phoenicians may have cultivated the vine around Marseilles even before this. By the early Middle Ages the production of wine on a large scale had become general. When Eleanor of Aquitaine, after having been Queen of France, became Queen of England the export trade from Bordeaux was firmly established. Regular sailings took place not only from there but also from the little port of Libourne, on the Dordogne, and these became a regular and important feature of Anglo-French trade and survived all the quarrels and even wars between the two countries.

In the latter part of the nineteenth century phylloxera arrived from the United States of America. Different varieties of the same insects attack different parts of the vine simultaneously. It proved impossible to destroy this all-powerful enemy and there came a moment when the whole of Europe faced the total extinction of its wine-making industry. Just in time, the idea of using American vine-stock, which is resistant to phylloxera, was put to the test and proved to be the answer to the appalling problem. Today the grafting of French grapes on American stocks is virtually universal in France. In some cases this caused a change in the nature of the wine produced and some once prosperous wine regions have not even yet fully recovered their lost importance.

The variety of grapes is enormous. Their choice and combination play a vital part in maintaining the quality of wines from particular areas: the Pinot-Chardonnay grape for white Burgundies; Pinots for Champagne and red Burgundies; Sémillon, Sauvignon, and Muscadelle for Bordeaux whites, Cabernets for Bordeaux and Loire reds, and the Chenin Blanc or Pineau de la Loire for Loire whites. These wines would be very much inferior to what they are at present if other grapes were used. The choice of varieties and the proportions used of each determine the quality and worth of each individual wine.

Tending the vineyard is an all-the-year-round task. The vines have to be fed frequently and amply, and the earth around their roots hoed almost incessantly. They have to be sprayed against attacks by virus diseases and various insect pests several times a year and, except in winter, have to be pruned again and again. Most French wine-producing vines are kept down to a height of not more than three feet. This makes the vintage a back-breaking job, as the best bunches always seem to be those nearest the ground. Young people with romantic visions of lazily plucking grapes from a series of vine-arbours would do well to think twice about taking a working holiday at vintage time on a French vineyard.

The weather is exactly right for the vintage only once in every ten or more years. It is a sobering thought that one severe frost at night at the wrong time of year – something to which the Loire valley is very liable – or a single day or night of hailstorms can mean a complete loss on a vineyard for an entire year.

This gives point to the possession of a number of vineyards in the same area but on slopes facing in different directions. They will all face the sun at some time of day, but the more they point different ways the less risk there is that all of them will be equally badly affected by adverse weather; there will always be some portion of the grape yield which will be saved.

Virtually all vineyards are on slopes, and a great many on stony ground, for the vine roots like to have something to grip. But to every rule which apparently governs the running of a successful vineyard there will be an exception or two. Vine and vineyard defy rigorous generalization.

In winter the vineyard itself with its formal military pattern of bare vines can be a stark sight, yet a few months later, at blossom time, the same vineyard will be a thing of glowing beauty. And when the vines are in full leaf the military array of the vines disappears, hidden in the profusion of the fresh-coloured green leaves. In the autumn the vineyard enters into visual glory, when the fierce colours of the turning leaves are supplemented by the reds or whites of the grape clusters awaiting the vintage, when the last pruning has cleared away such leaves as cast shadows on and kept the sunshine off the fruit.

Each year, in most cases, up to one-fifth of a vineyard is re-planted. With this yearly re-birth, a vineyard touches the edge of eternity.

Route I: ─────────────────

A Western Route from the Channel Ports to the Bay of Biscay and the Spanish Frontier

If you take a map of France and draw a line across it from La Baule on the estuary of the river Loire to Sedan on France's north-eastern frontier, you will find the line points almost exactly north-east and south-west. It divides France into two significantly different parts. North of the line the vine does not flourish and no wine is made. This used not to be the case, but either the climate has changed since medieval days, or the taste for the sour wines likely to have been produced has disappeared as improvements in transport have brought wines from better areas into wine shops all over France. This vine-deprived area accounts for approximately one-eighth of the area of the whole country.

All the French vineyards are now south of the line and between them produce hundreds of different wines. This book's five routes are concerned only with the wine-producing seven-eighths of the country and locate for the reader the areas in which particular wines are produced. Each route deals with any great wines to be met with on the way, but is mainly concerned with lesser wines worth the drinking, less well known, seldom written about, and always cheaper.

On Route I, if you are coming from any of the Channel ports and heading southwards and westwards, you will be almost at Nantes, on the Loire, before you reach wine country, for you will already have gathered (and in any case probably knew it beforehand) that no route from any of the ports will lead immediately to neat vineyards bearing the promise of a refreshing little local wine or opening up the prospect of enjoying a great one in its own surroundings.

The very first wine on this western route is not an outstanding one. All around Nantes, on both sides of the Loire, you will observe square patches of vineyard. From these comes the now popular but still inexpensive *Muscadet (appellation contrôlée)*. It is a pale white wine, made from the grape of this name which grows on not particularly fertile soil. There is in fact a second *A.C.* covering the Muscadet wines grown in the district known as the Sèvre-et-Maine and along the Coteaux-de-la-Loire. They are perhaps of a slightly higher quality. They rate 10° of alcohol against 9.5^o.

Muscadet, being a product of a single variety of grape, differs less than some wines from year to year. Though not excessively dry, it does hold a certain sharpness which makes it particularly suitable for drinking with fish and shellfish. It is also one of the few wines which will stand up to vinegary dishes, so any patriotic Briton who insists on eating his favourite fish and chips in France, well doused in vinegar, now knows of at least one wine which will not be entirely killed by the dish. Locally it is drunk with anything and everything. The average Frenchman does not take two or three wines with every meal — those days are long past — and Muscadet is very popular as a single wine to take all through a meal. It is drunk young and fresh, as it does not age well. Its lightness, sharpness, and cool colour make it particularly attractive on a hot, sunny day.

Muscadet with more than two years in bottle is probably best avoided, for then its attractive tang begins to disappear and nothing takes its place.

There is one other wine in this immediate region, the *Gros-Plant-du-Pays-Nantais*. It is a *V.D.Q.S.* wine *(vin délimité de qualité supérieure*: see the list of wine words at the beginning of the book). This unusual wine, made from the grape of the same name, is the object of a cult in certain circles in France, generally young ones. It is the "in" thing to prefer it, or to pretend to prefer it, to Muscadet. It is much sharper than Muscadet and, being made from a much coarser grape, a much coarser wine. It is white, with a definitely greenish tinge, and is drunk as young as or even younger than the Muscadets. It has one immense advantage — it costs less than a Muscadet, but it is difficult to find any other virtue in this thin, vinegary product of the vine. It grows only in the area immediately around the city of Nantes. The area has been extended comparatively recently to include the remain-

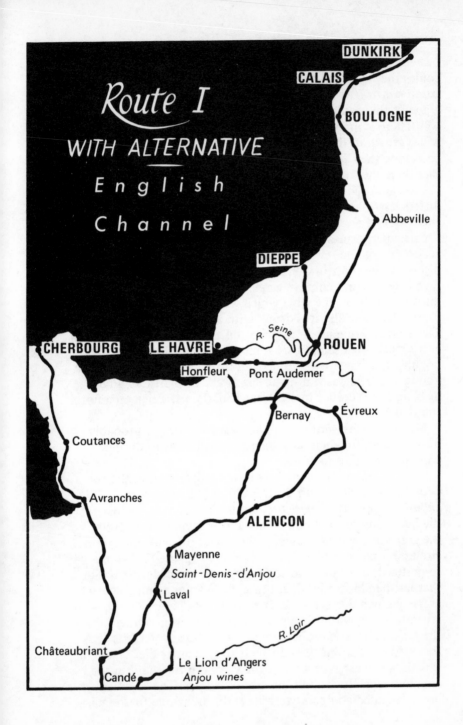

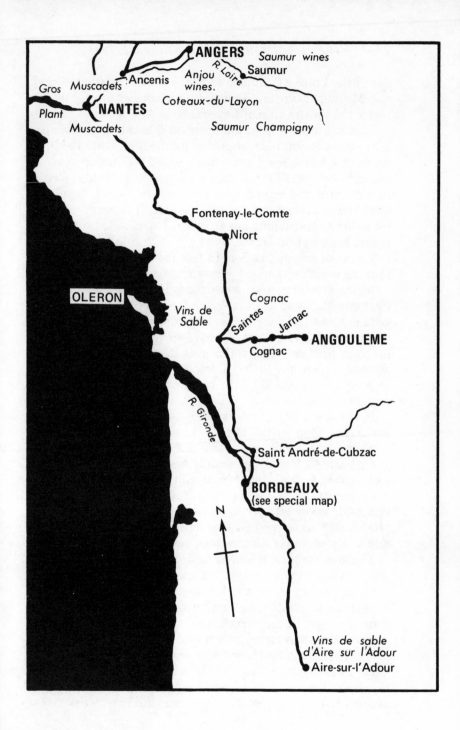

der of the Loire-Atlantique, in which Nantes is situated, and also Maine-et-Loire and Vendée: these wines can only be sold under the shorter title of *Gros-Plant*.

Immediately south of the Loire on this extreme western route there is not much choice of local wines. Once the little wines of *Fontenay-le-Comte* had a sound reputation as reliable *vins de pays (V.P.)*, then some producers introduced hybrid vines, and though quantity came in by one door, quality was pushed out through another. It is possible that something approaching one-fifth of French wine-production comes from hybrid grapes, but they are forbidden for use in any wine of any distinction. In fact their juice enters only into the most ordinary of *vins ordinaires*.

As the traveller comes southwards into Charente and Charente-Maritime he discovers vast areas of vineyards, yet virtually no table wine comes from them. Nearly the entire production of wine from these grapes is the thin, white product, hard and acid, which goes to nearby Cognac for distillation into the finest of brandies. It is very ironic that so poor a wine should be the basis for the aristocrat of the brandy world.

In common with all spirits, *Cognac* matures only in cask and not at all in bottle. There is a substantial loss through evaporation from the casks, and these have to be filled up every year. A "Napoleon" brandy is simply brandy from a cask started in the time of Napoleon of which a proportion has been drawn off and a proportion has evaporated and the two made good with young spirit ever since. Mostly the "Napoleon" concerned is never defined or given a date. It refers almost universally to Napoleon III.

The area from La Rochelle to Bordeaux provides something highly original: a fortified grape-juice apéritif with its own *appellation contrôlée*. It is not easy to find it outside its own area, through my own introduction to it was in a little ski resort in the French Alps.

The village was giving a reception for its visitors, which was presided over by the Mayor, who was also the village doctor. I asked him what, as a medical man, he himself drank on these occasions, knowing the French medical profession's general dislike of aperitifs. His own choice was this *Pineau des*

Charentes. He explained to me that it was the must of grapes fortified with brandy — Cognac brandy — which also prevented it from fermenting and becoming wine. He assured me that if one was obliged for social reasons to take an aperitif *Pineau des Charentes* was certainly the least harmful.

Pineau des Charentes takes its name from the fine Pineau grape which provides the must, and is sold either as a white or as a rosé. The grapes for the must are pressed very lightly early in the vintage, and never more than twenty-four hours after being picked. The Cognac used to "stop" and fortify the juice has to be *rassis*, that is either from the most recent distillation or from one immediately preceding the most recent. After fortification, the liquid has an overall alcoholic strength of not less than 16.5° nor more than 22°. It is then "rested" in barrel for a period of four months before being fined and drawn off. Only oak casks may be used. Finally, Pineau des Charentes may be sold only in sealed bottles.

Whatever may be the advantages and disadvantages of Pineau des Charentes, I find it delicious and above all comparison with its highly industrialized rivals from other parts of France.

Beyond the two Charentes the traveller quickly reaches Bordeaux. The immense choice of wines and the differences between them make the Bordelais unsuitable to be dealt with in the course of following a route. The wines of Bordeaux therefore have a complete chapter of their own later in the book.

Our route begins again on the southern side of Bordeaux, and after the better wines of this great area (some of the less good ones are not all that good) the next *V.P.* along it is by way of being an anti-climax. It is the *Vin-de-Sable* of the *département* of the Landes, of which the best individual specimen comes from Aire-sur-l'Adour. The first sight of a vineyard in this area, if one has not been advised beforehand, is likely to create a strong feeling of disbelief. The improbability of the vine flourishing in such sandy wastes is certainly very great. Nevertheless, the vine can be as accommodating in some places as it is unaccommodating in others. It does succeed in producing wine grapes from this impoverished soil. The wine made from these grapes has a flavour all its own.

It reminds me of the occasion, true or invented, when British gourmets invited Curnonsky to London. Curnonsky was once considered (even by so knowledgeable an expert as himself) to be the world's most authoritative gourmet. The object of the exercise was to observe his reaction to that celebrated English dish, Surrey capon with bread sauce. The chosen restaurant was Simpson's in the Strand.

The exciting moment came when Curnonsky, fork at the ready, was about to taste that barbaric accompaniment to poultry, English bread sauce. With bated breath his hosts saw him take it on his fork, put it into his mouth, and chew it with expressionless face. They waited for the devastating comment they all expected. All they got was, *"C'est curieux; c'est très curieux."* That was all the comment he would ever make about it.

That is how I feel about the Vin-de-Sable — it is curious; it is very curious. It is sharp and thin, and often almost colourless. And yet it has a strange attraction, so that having probably pulled a face at the first sip, one ends by taking a second glass. It could perhaps best be described as a gentler, more refined version of Gros-Plant.

There is another wine grown in the Landes and in Gers, *Tursan*. Its three varieties, white, red, and rosé, are covered by a *V.D.Q.S.* attribution. They are made from some unusual grapes and are fairly strong (white and red, 10.5^{O}, rosé 11°) and all have a flavour which is unusual rather than lovable.

Earlier on the route, on the island of Oléron, there is another Vin-de-Sable; the vineyards (very small) are most opportunely situated opposite the point on the mainland where the oyster-beds of Marennes flourish. Marennes oysters have never tasted quite as good as when eaten within minutes of being lifted out of their bed, and accompanied by the light, bone-dry, and unsophisticated Vin-de-Sable of the offshore island.

From the Landes to the Pyrenees the wines belong to Route II, but before describing them there is a longer variant to Route I which offers advantages well worth considering.

ROUTE I – VARIANT

From Calais and the northern ports generally an agreeable and largely traffic-free route to Nantes is via Evreux and Bernay to Alençon, Mayenne, and Laval, and then by the river bank to Nantes and the mouth of the Loire.

On this variant the vineyards begin at Mayenne in a very modest way with those of Saint-Denis-d'Anjou, where a red *vin-de-pays* is produced, a little earthy but a little superior to the run of *ordinaires*. But once Ancenis is reached one meets a rich selection of Muscadet and Gros-Plant from downstream, the fine growths of Anjou from upstream, and the *Coteaux-d'Ancenis* from around the little town itself. The red and rosé versions of this *V.D.Q.S.* wine are very similar to other reds and rosés of Anjou, but the white tastes of one of its less usual components, the juice of the Malvoisie grape. The name brings back memories of *There's a tavern in the town,* of W. H. Bellamy's *Simon the Cellarer* who, as you will remember, kept "a rare store of malmsey and malvoisie" (which, incidentally, are the same thing), and of English wine-drinking habits from Shakespeare's day through the Restoration to well into the nineteenth century. This grape would appear to have been introduced into France from Greece. It would be interesting to know how the Loire-side *Malvoisie* compared with the probably tougher *Malmsey* from Turkey and Greece. It would almost certainly have been gentler, though no doubt fortified like its rivals to stand the sea journey.

Among the many wines of Anjou there are no fewer than eighteen *appellations contrôlées* and it is as well to concentrate on them as they are sold at reasonable prices. Those that are sold under the generic name of *Anjou* do not differ very much from each other, but those that come under the heading of a smaller area are usually of a little higher quality and price.

The basic generic *A.C.* is simply *Anjou*, which covers white wines of a strength of 9.5° and red wines of a strength of 10°. Under this heading come a number of sub-headings, beginning with *Rosé-d'Anjou* (9°). A second sub-heading is for *Saumur* white and red (both 10°). The third sub-heading is for *Anjou-en-pétillant blanc,* a semi-sparkling white wine (9.5°), the

fourth for *Saumur pétillant blanc* (10°), and the last is for
the *Rosé-d'Anjou pétillant* (9.5°).

In general terms all these wines have a powerful flavour,
the whites being better than the reds and, in the opinion of
most people, the rosés being the best of the three. On the
whole they are not wines which age with any benefit and are
best drunk young and fresh. They are a little on the sweet
side in many cases, but this is a very variable feature. All are
sound, agreeable table wines, and all very good value.

The next *A.C.* is *Anjou-Rosé-de-Cabernet* which also covers
Saumur-Rosé-de-Cabernet. Both wines, at 11°, are definitely
stronger in alcohol than any of the previous ones, and keep
better and taste better for it. Whereas the Rosé-d'Anjou can
be the product of no less than six varieties of grape, these
Rosé-de-Cabernet wines are made exclusively from two varieties only of the splendid Cabernet grape, and the difference
in flavour is very great. These are certainly very good wines.

Made from the same two Cabernet grapes, and even more
powerful than the Anjou-Rosé-de-Cabernet (12°), are the
wines covered by the *A.C. Anjou-Coteaux-de-la-Loire-Rosé-
de-Cabernet*. Do not be put off by its enormously long name,
for this is one of the very best of all rosé wines.

Last of the Anjou *A.C.* with an uncomfortably long name
is *Anjou-Coteaux-de-la-Loire,* covering 12° white wines of
pleasant flavour but not any real distinction.

The last *A.C.* of all to include the word Anjou is *Anjou-
mousseux,* with which is linked *Saumur-mousseux,* both
deriving from a number of different grapes. These sparkling
wines are very popular in France, but are too sweet and too
undistinguished in flavour for my personal taste.

Though the name "Anjou" has disappeared, there remains
one *A.C.* for wines growing in the heart of the province along
the banks of the Loire. These are the best white wines of
Anjou, and hardly to be bettered along the whole length of
the Loire, the wines of *Savennières.* They are white wines
with a distinguished bouquet, made exclusively from the
Chenin-blanc grape, and rating 12.5° of alcoholic strength.
The two best vineyards are La Roche-aux-Moines and
Château-d'Epire, with the Coulée-de-Serrant running them a

very close third . . . and some knowledgeable people would
reverse that order.

Another very good-quality white wine to remember is
covered by the *A.C. Coteaux-du-Layon,* the Layon being a
small tributary of the Loire. These sweet and splendid wines
are made exclusively from Chenin-blanc grapes (also known
as Pinot-de-la-Loire), late-gathered, and again show the fre-
quent superiority of one-grape wines over some of the others.
It is a powerful wine (12°) of unforgettable and rich flavour,
redolent of the grape, strong in colour, giving equal pleasure
to the eye, the nose, and the palate.

The red wines of Anjou, as I have already mentioned, are
not the equal of the whites and rosés, but to all general-
izations there are exceptions. The exceptional red wine is
Souzay-Champigny or *Saumur-Champigny,* always known
locally as just *Champigny.* It is a wine which, without being
a great wine, is one of good colour, fair strength (10°), and
delightful flavour. Even locally it is not easy to find, and I
came across it not far from its own vineyards at one of the
two admirable restaurants of Les Rosiers, a charming village
of the right bank of the Loire, about half-way between
Saumur and Angers. As the *Michelin Guide* has it, when re-
commending a restaurant, "worth a detour".

Here this variant leaves Ancenis and its neighbourhood for
the short journey westwards along the right bank of the Loire
to join the original Route I at Nantes.

Route II:

*A Route to the Central Pyrenees by Roads
running to the West of the Massif Central*

Even though it did not exactly hug the coast, Route I kept well to the west. Route II runs more inland, and a variant to part of it approaches the foothills of the central mountain area.

By this route the first good wine is found soon after Le Mans has been left behind. It is a white wine with an *appellation contrôlée* of its own, Jasnières. It is also a historic grape, for it is mentioned by name in a charter dated as early as A.D. 845. Without wishing to deprive the grape of any glory, it must be said that nearly all charters of the ninth century are forgeries establishing and confirming doubtful claims to church property. If this is the case the forgery itself would in all probability be not later than the twelfth century (the great century for such forgeries) which yet gives the grape a very long record. It is perhaps a little surprising to find it still in use after all these centuries, for in terms of quantity it is a poor producer and matures late in the season. However, "quality will tell", and no other grape growing on the soil of the vineyards of either side of the Loire gives quite such a clear, clean wine with such a clear, clean taste. It does just this for the wine of Jasnières.

After Jasnières good *Coteaux-du-Loir (A.C.)* wines are to be found along this route. The 10° whites are made only from Chenin-blanc grapes and are good, while the 9.5° reds made from a medley of grapes are not quite their equal.

At Tours one finds the red, rosé, and white wines coming under the generic *appellation contrôlée* of *Touraine,* which includes *pétillant* versions. The white is a blend of different grapes which may or may not include a proportion of Chenin and the reds are an even more complicated mixture, the former giving 9.5° and the latter 9° of alcoholic strength.

They are quite sound and drinkable, these Touraine wines, but not particularly interesting. Of the three, the rosé seems to be the local preference. Wines sold under this same *A.C.* as *Touraine-Azay-le-Rideau* have a little more body and flavour than those sold just as "Touraine", and this is also true of *Touraine-Amboise* and *Touraine-Mesland*, which are perhaps a shade coarser.

Although not rivalling Saumur-mousseux in popularity, *Touraine-mousseux* is very widely sold, and has a separate *A.C.* of its own. Obviously the French like these sweet sparkling wines, but it is doubtful if they have much of a following among the British. In Britain, of course, it pays the same exorbitant duty as Champagne, though why a wine that bubbles should be taxed almost off the market as compared with one that does not is inexplicable.

From this part of the Loire come distinguished red wines under their own *appellations contrôlées*. These are the wines of *Bourgueil* and *Saint-Nicolas-de-Bourgueil* from the north side of the river, and *Chinon* from the south side. To be more exact Chinon is produced on both banks of the river Vienne just before it flows into the Loire from the south. It was loudly praised by Rabelais, the writer and learned physician with whose ideas on diet we have only recently caught up. He ended his life as parish priest of Meudon, near Paris, famous for his books of earthy humour. Praise of the wines from the vineyards of Chinon, his native town, abound – but not a single reference is made to the near-by rivals, the wines of Bourgueil. Such is local patriotism!

Saint-Nicolas-de-Bourgueil is more strictly limited in terms of permitted production per hectare than is neighbouring Bourgueil, and the wines of the former are considered slightly better. Both have a 9.5° alcoholic strength, as has Chinon. All three are wines of very full flavour, a curious, flower-scented bouquet, and a very deep colour. There is little to choose between the three, with the Bourgueils having perhaps slightly the stronger texture. There is a difference in flavour, admittedly, but it would be difficult to describe what it is. The red is the most widely known, but in both cases a rosé is also produced, and in the case of Chinon a white wine as

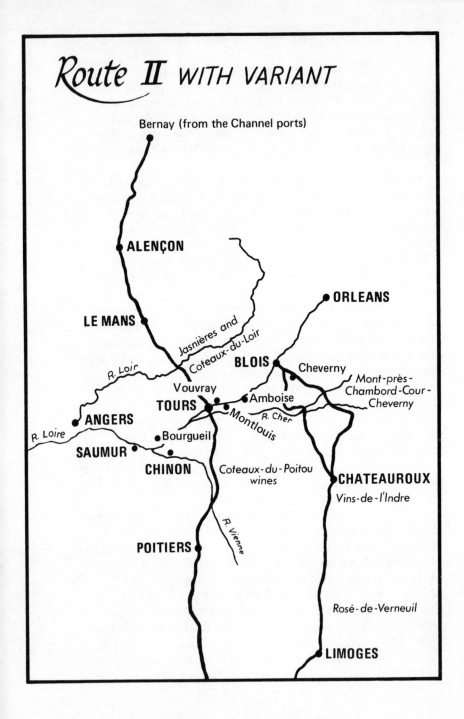

Route II WITH VARIANT

Bernay (from the Channel ports)

ALENÇON

LE MANS

ORLEANS

Jasnières and Coteaux-du-Loir

R. Loir

BLOIS

Cheverny

Mont-près-Chambord-Cour-Cheverny

Vouvray

Amboise

TOURS

Montlouis

R. Cher

R. Loire

ANGERS

Bourgueil

SAUMUR

CHINON

Coteaux-du-Poitou wines

CHATEAUROUX

Vins-de-l'Indre

R. Vienne

POITIERS

Rosé-de-Verneuil

LIMOGES

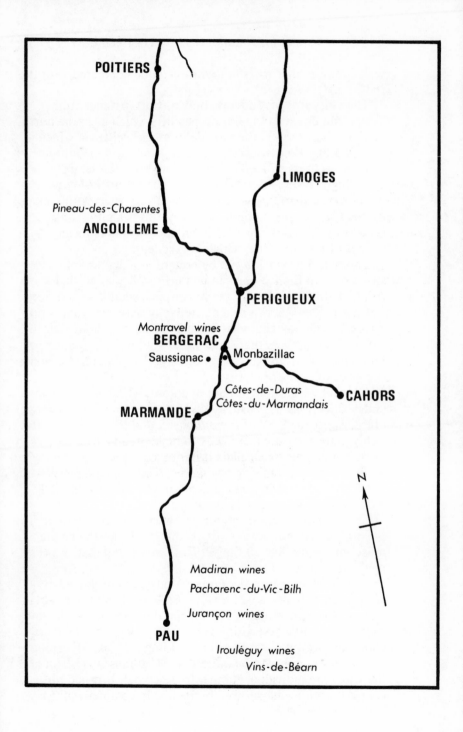

well – but neither rosés nor whites can be compared with the reds.

The vineyards of Vouvray, only a short distance from Tours, run down to the limestone cliffs which edge the north bank of the Loire. These provide immense cellars in which the sparkling *Vouvray* is stored. The Vouvray *appellation contrôlée* covers still wines (plain Vouvray), the semi-sparkling *Vouvray-en-pétillant,* and the famous *Vouvray-mousseux,* a sparkling wine made (and very successfully made) by the Champagne method. In a way this is a pity, for the success of the sparkling version blinds consumers to the virtues of the still wine, which is excellent.

The sparkling version can be bought as a dry wine or as a sweet one. In France one can be fairly well assured that a bottle marked "Vouvray" really contains what it says it does, but there does seem to be a discrepancy between what is produced at Vouvray and what is consumed throughout the world. One suspects that some wines sold outside France contain wine that is not all from Vouvray, if any at all, this being the price of over-popularity.

The still wine is a light gold in colour, with some intriguing green reflections. It is usually on the sweet side, quite strong (11° against the 9.5° of the *mousseux* and the *pétillant*), and richly grape-flavoured. It needs to be kept, and after two years or so in the limestone cellars it improves immensely from what are, frankly, unpromising beginnings. Today's tendencies being entirely towards drinking wines at an ever earlier age, really well-matured Vouvray has become scarce.

The *pétillant* version should, of course, be drunk young, for these wines are not always very stable. It tickles the palate most amusingly, like all the *pétillant* wines, and makes a very pleasant change.

A somewhat paler reflection of Vouvray is produced at *Montlouis.* It is also a white wine produced from Chenin-blanc grapes. It is lighter than Vouvray and does not age in the same way. In fact, it is best drunk very young. Here too the wine comes in three ways, still, semi-sparkling, and sparkling, and all the wines appear to be quite dry. Montlouis is an *A.C.,* and the wines are individual enough to deserve it. If it had not been so much overshadowed by its highly commercialized neighbour Montlouis might well have had a more widespread reputation.

Apart from all these choicer wines, there are many *vins de pays* to be found up and down the Loire. The best of them come under the label *Coteaux-de-Touraine*. All of them are sold in the traditional three forms, red, rosé, and white. According to local inhabitants, those grown around *Saché*, *Joué-lès-Tours* (as a possibly useful piece of information, *lès* in a French place name means "near"), *Saint-Avertin*, *Lussault*, and *Nazelles* are the ones to be preferred. All these wines are very inexpensive and honest, but not really very interesting.

The main direction of this route is now southwards, and there are few wines of merit to detain or delight the traveller until he finds himself on the eastern border of the kingdom of Pineau-des-Charentes (see Route I) which stretches out to just a little below Angoulême. The unpretentious *Coteaux-du-Poitou* are *vins de pays* of interest only because they mark the extreme limit of the influence of soil and climate of the Loire. They give way in the Périgord to others much richer and more memorable.

The wines of *Bergerac* have a long-standing connection with Britain. The region was part of the dowry of the formidable Queen Eleanor of Aquitaine when, having been divorced by the King of France, she married the fiery young Count of Anjou. When he became King Henry II of England and Eleanor became Queen of England she fostered the import of wines from her own domains in France. Regular shipments of Bordeaux wines from Libourne began, chiefly the wines of *Saint-Emilion*, but the wines of Bergerac were preferred even to these.

Between 1875 and 1885, the Bergerac vineyards were utterly devastated by phylloxera and, with those of *Cahors*, proved to be the heaviest sufferers in all France. When the situation was saved, *in extremis*, by the planting of American root stock and the grafting on of French wine grapes, Bergerac had been so heavily infested that it was many years before it was felt worth while to undertake this quite costly process. The new *Bergerac* wines, therefore, are still very recent in origin, and probably not very much like those which made this name famous all through the Middle Ages and later. The *appellation contrôlée* which includes them is *Côtes-de-Bergerac,* but there are others covering individual wines. They are all powerful wines. *Bergerac-rouge* and *Bergerac-rosé* both have an 11⁰ minimum of alcoholic content and the white *Bergerac-Côtes-de-Saussignac* has a minimum of no less than 12⁰. The whites are sweet to much the same degree that Sauternes are sweet. The reds are full-bodied, soft, and pleasant to drink. In earlier years these wines were rather rough; in recent years they have been much improved and at least one of them has reached a high degree of perfection. This is *Monbazillac,* one of those mentioned above which has an *A.C.* of its own.

Monks cleared the land and planted the first vineyards on the hills above the plain of the Dordogne in 1510. Thus began Monbazillac, then as now a carefully prepared white wine. Today, like many of the French sweet white wines, it is made from Sauvignon, Muscadelle, and Sémillon grapes. As in the Sauternes area, they are allowed to remain on the vine until the skins wrinkle and crack. The now thick, sugar-laden juice oozes through minute cracks in the skin. The parasitic mould *Botrytis cinerea* settles on the grape, thrusts its microscopic roots through the cracks, absorbs much of the water in the juice, and alters its physical composition. The juice naturally becomes thicker from the loss of water and in some way still mysterious becomes enriched by this mould which the French call *la pourriture noble,* "the noble rot". The world-celebrated wines of *Château-d'Yquem,* for example, depend entirely upon this grey-green, powdery, microscopic organism for their perfection. The slightest touch, the lightest wind, will send it floating away in the air so that it spreads in disordered patterns, coating some grapes entirely and missing others. At vintage time the grape-gatherers search for the brownest and most disagreeable-looking grapes. They come back time and time again until the very last of the grapes have been fully worked upon by the miracle mould.

This is the way Monbazillac is made. So greatly has it improved in later years that it is no longer out of place to compare it with the fine Barsacs. Its sugary juice will only vinify in a cellar with a strict temperature range of 54°F. mimimum to 60°F. maximum (12°C. to 15°C.). Care is taken not to allow all the sugar to turn to alcohol but to retain sufficient to make Monbazillac one of the most delicious of sweet white wines. The sugar that is converted gives it an alcoholic strength of 13°, like the Barsacs which are made in the same way from the same grapes.

Before being bottled, Monbazillac is aged for two years in oak casks, and then will naturally go on improving with age in bottle. I would not pretend that Monbazillac has all the fine characteristics of the best Barsacs, but it is gradually creeping up on them.

Still in this area, the wines of *Montravel, Côtes-de-Montravel,* and *Haut-Montravel,* all whites, are made from the same grapes as Monbazillac, but are less sweet and not of the same supreme quality: they are also less alcoholic. Montravel has a minimum 10.5° and the other two 12°. *Rosette* is another of the rich whites with an independent *A.C.* (12°) and *Pécharmant* (also with its own *A.C.*) is the pleasantest of all the red wines of the area (11°).

The white Bergerac wines should be avoided at lunch-time by travellers who are going on driving after their meal. They go down so easily and so pleasingly that it is all too easy to forget their strength. Conversely, they are magnificent to drink in the evening when the day's driving is over.

Southwards still from Bergerac one comes to the wines of the *Côtes-de-Duras (A.C.),* both white (10.5°) and red (10°). Considerable quantities, mainly of white, are produced but neither are very exciting and after the Bergerac wines seem somewhat devoid of flavour. As one goes farther into this area the wines become even duller. The *Côtes-du-Marmandais* are predominantly white *V.D.Q.S.* wines, with a little red also made, and this is equally true of the *Côtes-de-Buzet V.D.Q.S.* There is little flavour or individuality about them, and all one can say is that they are acceptable in an area in which no outstanding wines are grown.

There is, however, a strange little *vin de pays* rejoicing in the improbable name of *Cocument,* the cause of a very great number of very bad jokes. For those who have little French,

cocu means "cuckold". There seems no valid reason to
accept the truth of the local story that in olden days a pair
of horns was presented to every purchaser of a bottle who
looked as if he might have earned them. The wine itself has
an earthy taste entirely in keeping with the type of humour
its name generates. Béarn, at the approaches to Pau, offers
two wines coming under a single *appellation contrôlée* −
Pacharenc-du-Vic-Bilh. The red wines coming under this *A.C.*
are those of *Madiran* (11°), with a rather odd, sweetish
flavour, but quite agreeable to drink. Far odder in flavour
are the white wines, sold as *Pacharenc-du-Vic-Bilh*. They are
the product of two very good grapes (Sémillon and
Sauvignon) and two much lesser ones (Ruffiac and Manseng),
rather sweet and, at 12°, powerful; the grapes are allowed to
become over-ripe before being pressed. I think this wine is an
acquired taste, but there has never been time to acquire it.
I am told that the wine, which has a rich colour and a powerful aroma, has quite extraordinary keeping powers, but I have
not been able to put this to the test.

Almost at Pau are the famous *Jurançon (A.C.)* vineyards.
Famous because the wine of Jurançon was used to wet the
infant lips of the new-born Henri of Navarre, who became
King Henri IV of France, and instituted this custom at the
Court of France: thereafter all boy babies born into the
royal family had their lips moistened with Jurançon as their
first introduction to wine, and almost to life itself.
Phylloxera, alas, devastated the Jurançon vineyards and they
have never recovered; today they occupy only a tiny area
compared with those of earlier times. And today the wine is
not the same. From the rich red wine which, according to
contemporary accounts, it used to be, it has become a white
one since American stock was introduced.

Today's Jurançon is the product of a mixture of little-
known grapes (Gros Manseng, Petit Manseng, Courbu,
Carmaralet, and Lauzet) and has a quite unique flavour. There
is an underlay of a most delicate flavour, which one comes
to recognize, but first acquaintance with this wine is likely to
prove disappointing. Once again, it would improve with long
years in bottle, but it is now drunk too young and old bottles
are increasingly difficult to find.

After the unusual charm of Jurançon the *V.D.Q.S.* wines of *Irouléguy,* red, rosé, and white, will inevitably seem a little dull; the red is the best. Then comes another *V.D.Q.S.*, the *Vin de Béarn,* which includes the *Rosé-de-Béarn* and the *Rousselet-de-Béarn,* which is a white wine made from the Roussette grape. Both are a little on the rough side, but reasonably good drinking and inexpensive. The best of the rosés is the one produced on the hills around Salies-Bellocq.

After this, as far as the Spanish frontier at Bourg-Madame, there are only *vins de pays,* and if any of them seem better than the others it is those of *Villefranque, Peyriguère, Pouyastrac, Sère, Roustaing,* and lastly, almost at journey's end, the agreeably fresh and unpretentious *Engraviès.*

ROUTE II – VARIANT

A good alternative route from Tours to Périgueux is to begin by moving up river from Tours to Blois, where one should be able to find the best wines of the *département* of Loir-et-Cher, the reds and the whites of *Saint-Romain (A.C.).* Both are made from high-grade grapes, the 10.5° reds from three of the best Pinot varieties, and the 11° whites from Pinot blanc and Chardonnay. Production must be quite small, for they are not to be found without inquiry, but both rank among the very best of the Loire valley wines, being of sound body, excellent flavour and bouquet, and agreeable colour.

From the immediate neighbourhood comes the contrasting wine, the white *V.D.Q.S. Mont-près-Chambord-Cour-Cheverny,* a name which leaves little room for anything else on the label. It is a fresh little wine, but it really doesn't live up to the standards of the two châteaux it names. After that we come down to *vins de pays.* They include *Coteaux-du-Blésois* and *Coteaux-du-Vendômois,* both whites, and the red, rosé, and white wines of *Montrichard* – all easy to drink but not at all memorable.

Then, travelling towards Châteauroux, come the *vins de l'Indre,* red and white *vins de pays* with a much less sophisticated flavour already to distinguish them from the wines of the Loire valley. Nearer to Limoges, however, there is a really very charming *Rosé-de-Verneuil* which, like all *vins de pays,* probably has as many bad years as it has good: at its best this is an unexpectedly pleasant wine to drink. And after that there is no other wine to come which will even remotely remind one of the fast-receding Loire. To compensate, though, the wines of the Dordogne in all their richness soon make their first appearance.

Route III:

A Route to the Mediterranean and the Spanish Frontier by Way of the Massif Central

Either Blois or Orléans makes a suitable starting-point for this route, according to one's point of arrival in France and whether Paris is to be included or avoided. It has to be admitted that neither the wines of the Blésois nor the Orléanais are particularly good specimens as an introduction to a wine-seeking journey, for here on the immense slow curve of the river Loire near Orléans its northernmost point is reached, and one must follow it farther to the south to reach the really first-class wines.

The *V.D.Q.S. vins de l'Orléanais* are red, rosé, and white, with a not very high alcohol content of 9° for the red and 10° for the white and rosé, but many much better wines rate no more than these figures. The wines lack body and bouquet and whatever virtues they have are in a minor key. Orléans is more famed for its wine vinegar than for its wine, but jokes on this subject, involving the interchangeability of the two, are locally considered to be in very bad taste.

As one rounds the bend of the river one arrives at Giens. The *Côtes-de-Gien* (or *Coteaux du Giennois*) are *V.D.Q.S.* red and white wines which also develop 9° and 10° of alcohol respectively. The reds are made from the juice of Gamay and Pinot grapes and are well flavoured, and the whites from Sauvignon and Chenin blanc, both first-class grapes definitely much to be preferred to the comparable Orléanais products.

It is not until the river has almost entirely straightened out again at the end of this stupendous curve that really high-class wines are to be found, at Pouilly. Two wines in fact are produced here, one very good indeed and the other not so good, and care must be taken not to get them confused. They both come under the same portmanteau *appellation, Pouilly-sur-Loire* and *Blanc-fumé-de-Pouilly* (or *Pouilly-fumé*). Both are

Route III

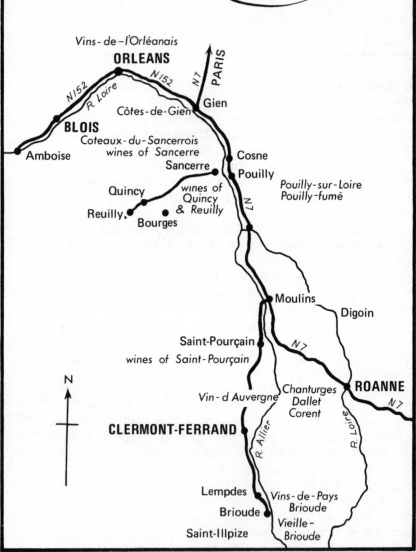

Vins - de - l'Orléanais

ORLEANS

N152

R. Loire

N152

N7

PARIS

Gien

Côtes - de - Gien

BLOIS

Coteaux - du - Sancerrois
wines of *Sancerre*

Amboise

Cosne

Sancerre

Pouilly

Pouilly - sur - Loire
Pouilly - fumé

Quincy

wines of
Quincy
& Reuilly

N7

Reuilly.

Bourges

Moulins

Digoin

Saint-Pourçain

N7

wines of Saint-Pourçain

N

ROANNE

Vin - d'Auvergne

Chanturges
Dallet
Corent

N7

CLERMONT-FERRAND

R. Allier

R. Loire

Lempdes

Vins - de - Pays
Brioude

Brioude

Vieille -
Brioude

Saint-Illpize

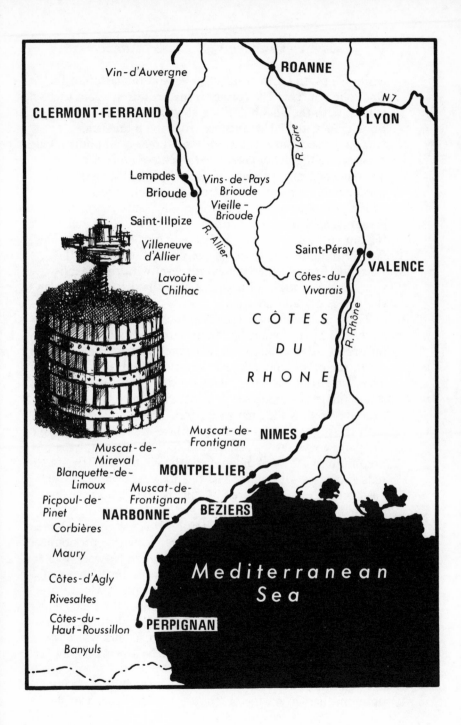

Vin-d'Auvergne

ROANNE

N 7

CLERMONT-FERRAND

LYON

R. Loire

Lempdes
Brioude

Vins-de-Pays
Brioude
Vieille-
Brioude

Saint-Illpize

Saint-Péray

VALENCE

Villeneuve
d'Allier

Côtes-du-
Vivarais

Lavoûte-
Chilhac

R. Allier

CÔTES

DU

RHONE

R. Rhône

Muscat-de-
Frontignan

NIMES

Muscat-de-
Mireval
Blanquette-de-
Limoux

MONTPELLIER

Picpoul-de-
Pinet

Muscat-de-
Frontignan

NARBONNE

BEZIERS

Corbières

Maury

Mediterranean
Sea

Côtes-d'Agly

Rivesaltes

Côtes-du-
Haut-Roussillon

PERPIGNAN

Banyuls

white wines, the former having a 9° and the latter an 11° alcoholic content. The former is made entirely from Chasselas grapes, with the possibility of a slight admixture of Blanc-fumé grapes, the latter entirely from the Blanc-fumé. As a consequence, the *Pouilly-sur-Loire* is an undistinguished wine, while the delicious *Blanc-fumé-de-Pouilly* is a rather distinguished one. In spite of its name it is not a kippered white wine. Its name comes from the smoky-white grape, which, when grown for the Graves and Sauternes of Bordeaux, is known as Sauvignon. It has a clear, light colour and a rich flavour to which it is easy to become greatly attached. This flavour reminds one rather vaguely that the bend of the Loire has brought these vineyards level with the Chablis vineyards of northern Burgundy, and the distance between the two is not all that great.

Three little wines are grown in these parts, all red *vins de pays,* and their flavour, like their names, recalls the deep, unsophisticated countryside: *Battanet, Riousse,* and *Sagoule.*

On the other bank (the left bank) of the Loire, in the *département* of the Cher, Sancerre stands on the top of a steep hill, overlooking the considerable vineyards which produced red, white, and rosé wines. The white is the one with the reputation, though the others are agreeable enough. They are covered by a *Sancerre A.C.* which lays down a minimum of 10.5° of alcohol for the whites and 10° for the reds and rosés. During the last twenty years white Sancerre has become much favoured by "in" people, who have discovered in it virtues which few outside the immediate area ever seem to have recognized before. It is a very good wine, made exclusively from Sauvignon grapes, with a pronounced and delicious flavour. It is best drunk when between two and five years old: it is not likely to improve in bottle beyond that. The unfashionable red too is an excellent wine, also made exclusively from one variety of grape, the Pinot noir which gives us Champagne and admirable red Burgundies.

The *Coteaux du Sancerrois* are red, rosé, and white *vins de pays* of very variable quality, with the best being highly drinkable.

Even more excellent than the *Sancerre* white is, in my opinion, the white wine of *Quincy (A.C.),* again a single-grape wine (Sauvignon) with a minimum 10.5^{O} of alcohol. This is a drier wine than *Sancerre*, very stylish, clear, and refreshing. Like Sancerre, it is best drunk after two years and before five years. It has recently become so popular that it is ever more difficult to find one older than two years, and some people are taking to drinking it when only a year old, which is a crime when just one extra year in bottle will transform it into something so much better.

To reach the Quincy vineyards one must turn one's back on the river Loire and go on through Bourges, and a few miles beyond. First one comes to the *Reuilly* vineyards, producing white, rosé, and red *A.C.* wines. These seem to me to have been too long underrated, even in France itself, and although Quincy, other things being equal, would always be my first choice, I would far sooner content myself with the wines of Reuilly than be forced into drinking a Quincy too young to be enjoyed. The 10.5^{O} Reuilly white is also made exclusively from Sauvignon grapes; the 10° rosé and red from Pinot noir and Pinot gris. These very good and inexpensive wines will come as a most pleasant surprise to visitors who have never met them before.

Returning from the Quincy vineyards to the right bank of the Loire, the route lies through Moulins and Clermont-Ferrand. The volcanic soil of Auvergne does not really lend itself to any very satisfactory growing of the vine, and the very cold winters do not help. However, there is a *V.D.Q.S. Côtes-d'Auvergne* (also known as *Vin-d'Auvergne*), in red, rosé, and white versions, hard and not all that well flavoured. Better known is the *V.D.Q.S. Saint-Pourçain-sur-Sioule*, red, rosé, white, and *gris* (see the list of wine words), but those I have tasted have not been very good. The dry white has certainly been the best of them. I am told that in the last few years a real effort has been made to give them a smoother texture and to reduce excessive acidity.

There are also some definitely bucolic *vins de pays*. The wines of *Chanturgues,* which is one of the names that comes to mind, were, it is asserted, beloved of Louis XIV. That was long before phylloxera ravaged the vineyards. The red wines of today can hardly resemble the royal favourite of so long ago. The red wines of Chanturgues and of *Dallet* and the white wines of *Corent* are just honest-to-goodness rough country wines, and as long as you expect nothing more you will not be disappointed.

Beyond Auvergne, the route runs through the Haute-Loire, a *département* which is not very rich in wines, or in anything else except old villages and townlets hardly touched by time, attractive little rivers, flowing in all directions, and beautifully green valleys. There are none but local wines, and though they have none of the finesse of the great wines which are only just a little farther on they do have a flavour which begins to suggest them.

The local wines are all reds. Local opinion points to *Brioude, Vieille-Brioude, Lempdes, Saint-Illpize, Villeneuve-d'Allier,* and *Lavoûte-Chilhac* as being the best of these *vins de pays.* The choice may not be totally unprejudiced, for the opinions are those, respectively, of the men of Brioude, Vieille-Brioude, Lempdes, Saint-Illpize, Villeneuve-d'Allier, and Lavoûte-Chilhac. The wines themselves are hard little reds from quite a hard countryside.

Moving from the Haute-Loire to the Ardèche, the wine situation changes entirely, for here, for the first time, we meet some of the wines of the Côtes-du-Rhône. This *appellation contrôlée* is a complicated and a very far-reaching one. It covers areas on both sides of the river Rhône, spread over six *départements* and measuring more than a hundred miles in length. From north to south, these *départements* are: Rhône, Loire, Drôme, Ardèche, Vaucluse, and Gard. The complications arise because the *appellation* can be both up-graded and down-graded by the addition of extra information to just its name. Furthermore, nine of the wines entitled to be called "Côtes-du-Rhône" have individual *appellations* as well.

Four of the six *départements* producing Côtes-du-Rhône wines are judged the most likely to fail to meet the strict requirements of the generic *appellation.* Their wines may, however, be sold as Côtes-du-Rhône provided that the name of the *département* is added to the generic name. Thus *Côtes-du-Rhône-Ardèche, Côtes-du-Rhône-Drôme, Côtes-du-Rhône-Loire,* and *Côtes-du-Rhône-Rhône* are less good than plain *Côtes-du-Rhône.* Whether for red, rosé, or white, the

Côtes-du-Rhône wines must contain 11° of alcohol. But when the generic name is followed by that of a *département,* the reds and rosés need be no stronger than 9.5°, and the whites 10°.

On the other hand when the generic "Côtes-du-Rhône" is followed by the name of a concise locality, the wines will be stronger. *Côtes-du-Rhône-Gigondas, Côtes-du-Rhône-Laudun, Côtes-du-Rhône-Vacquéras,* and *Côtes-du-Rhône-Vinsobres,* whether white, red, or rosé, must rate not less than 12.5° — these are very powerful table wines. Those of *Cairanne* must not be less than 12° and the same figure applies to the rosés of *Chusclan* — the only ones made.

These stronger wines are collectively but quite unofficially known as *Côtes-du-Rhône-Villages.* To summarize in a single sentence: the best wines are those which bear a village name after the title of the *appellation;* those that bear the appellation without any addition are just a little less strong; those that bear the name of one of the four *départements* after the title are the weakest in alcoholic strength and therefore the least likely to age well.

What are they like, these wines from this vast area? They are lighter than the more luscious burgundies of the Côte-d'Or. They are perhaps a little reminiscent of the Beaujolais, though the flavour is quite different. They are mostly reds, but the few whites include some of the very finest in France.

To return to the Ardèche before following the route farther to the west and south, the fine red wines of *Cornas (A.C.)* are similar to, but having more body and a little greater alcoholic strength than, the much more famous ones of Hermitage from the other side of the river (10.5° as compared with 10°). They deserve to be better known than they are.

Just to the south of the Cornas vineyards come those of *Saint-Péray* which produce a most delightful white wine. It is only moderately strong (10°) but a most attractive one, comparable with the white Hermitage wines from across the river, but a little lighter in texture. It is prepared both as a still wine and as a *mousseux.* I believe it to be the most attractive sparkling wine in France after Champagne. Others may prefer Vouvray or Saumur, Gaillac or Blanquette de Limoux, but I find this *mousseux* of Saint-Péray — light, dry, and beautifully limpid — to have a more delicate flavour than its near rivals.

Saint-Joseph also has an individual *A.C.* for its 10° red and white wines. The reds come nearer to Moulin-à-Vent and Morgon than they do to the other wines of this *département*, but they are comparatively little known, though not less to be appreciated.

Inevitably, after this array of very good wines, those below the *A.C.* level come as an anti-climax. The best are the *Côtes-du-Vivarais (V.D.Q.S.)*. Red, white, and rosé are produced from a variety of grapes. All are rated at 10.5^O of alcohol, or 11° if the generic title is followed by the name of a *cru*. They are quite sound wines, but dull in flavour when taken after the excellent Côtes-du-Rhône.

On leaving the Ardèche the route next enters the *département* of the Gard, in which we find a continuation of the Côtes-du-Vivarais and also of the Côtes-du-Rhône, the latter beginning with a name widely known, *Tavel-rosé*, which has its own *appellation contrôlée*. It is by no means entirely thanks to its intelligent marketing that it is a famous wine. Coming as it does from these southern parts it is necessarily dry and, on the whole, a little hard — a man's wine essentially, one would have thought. In fact it has a powerful feminine following, perhaps not only from its flavour but in part from the definitely feminine appeal of its colour. It is quite strong (11°) and ages well for a rosé.

The rosé wines of *Lirac (A.C.)* are the sisters of those of Tavel, but even stronger (11.5^O). Although so similar and of an equally high quality they are far less well known. The *appellation* refers also to *Lirac* red and white wines, but neither have come my way. The powerful *Côtes-du-Rhône-Chusclan* (12°) is another of these very good, strong rosé wines of excellent flavour and, as we have already seen, the designation places it above the plain Côtes-du-Rhône.

Finally in the Gard there is one *V.D.Q.S.*, the red or white *Costières-du-Gard*, a pair which stand up well to highly fla-voured Provencal food.

From the Gard the route goes westwards into the *département* of the Hérault, which in terms of quantity is one of the great wine-producing areas in France. Indeed, an almost unbroken sequence of vineyards extends westwards well beyond this *département* and right up to the Pyrenees and the Spanish frontier. This domination of the vine – amounting over a very wide area to being almost a monoculture – has been fought by successive French Governments ever since the War, and with some success. Orchards for early fruit and fields for early vegetables have replaced a proportion of the endless vineyards. Even the transfer of oyster spat from beds in the Bay of Biscay to the plankton-rich lagoons of Languedoc has been successful, and the little *V.P.* wine of *Marseillan* has found a new outlet as a wine to accompany the oysters.

It would be idle to pretend to be able to deal accurately and completely with each one of the many wines of Languedoc. Frankly, many of them hardly deserve a mention, and of those that do a number are so similar that it is all but impossible to distinguish between them. The area produces immense quantities of second-rate wines which are blended and then sold throughout the country by co-operatives and wholesale wine merchants. Good blending certainly improves them but, though there is nothing particularly wrong with them, they are just lacking in interest. Great quantities go to the making of vermouth, for which the centre is Cète, and to other wine-based French aperitifs, in the neighbourhood of Béziers.

Nevertheless, there are wines which have an individual interest, and these are listed below. First come the *A.C.* wines described as "natural sweet wines" *(vins doux naturels),* which in spite of their name are not entirely left in their natural state, but are fortified with 90° alcohol to an extent of not less than 5 per cent in volume and not more than 15 per cent, and those described as "dessert wines" *(vins de liqueur)* which are fortified in the same way but more heavily, the minimum being 15 per cent of added 90° alcohol. Most of these wines are produced entirely or in part from muscat grapes, have a powerful flavour, and are very mellow and sweet, which tends to disguise their alcoholic strength in a somewhat treacherous manner. Even the least distinguished of these wines can be very good if allowed to age sufficiently. Taken highly chilled (no amount of chilling will kill their powerful flavour) they make an excellent aperitif, which is their common use in Languedoc itself. They include:

Frontignan and *Muscat de Frontignan*
Muscat de Lunel
Muscat de Mireval
Muscat de Saint-Jean-de-Minervois

Then come the table wines, of which only the *Clairette-du-Languedoc* has an *A.C.* This is a white wine, made from the Clairette grape, sweet and pleasant, of a very light yellow colour with green reflections. It has a *rancio* version, which supposedly makes it taste like Madeira. It is made from over-ripe grapes and must age for at least three years before being sold. This Spanish word indicates a well-aged and mellow wine which, with age, becomes almost intolerably sweet to some tastes. The table wines lose any greenish tinge they may have had, and go a deeper and sometimes browny yellow, while the dessert wines come to look the colour of tawny port. After this one *A.C.* wine, we come to the whole range of *V.D.Q.S.* wines, which means that at least they should be constant in their quality:

Cabrières, 11° rosé
Coteaux-de-la-Méjanelle, 11.5° reds, 11° whites
Coteaux-de-Saint-Christol, 11° red and rosé
Coteaux-de-Vérargues, 11° red and rosé

These four also come under a generic *Coteaux-du-Languedoc* title, which includes:

La Clape, 11° reds and whites and rosés
Faugères, 11° reds and whites
Pic-Saint-Loup, 11° reds, whites, and rosés
Quatourze, 11° reds, whites, and rosés
Saint-Chinian, 11° reds
Saint-Drézery, 11° reds
Saint-Georges-d'Orques, 11° reds
Saint-Saturnin with *Montpeyroux,* 11° reds and rosés

Outside the Coteaux-du-Languedoc there are two others which are produced in this part of the world. First there is the *V.D.Q.S. Minervois*, 10° reds and 11° whites, and rosés of a better quality than most of the other Languedoc wines. This title also covers the *Vin-Noble-du-Minervois* or *Minervois-noble*, powerful red, white, and rosé wines, all running to not less than 13° of alcohol. These are much esteemed in France.

Our last wine in the Hérault is the strangely named *Picpoul-de-Pinet*, which is sometimes written *Piquepoult-de-Pinet*. This is taken from the name of a grape, the grape which gives most of the flavour to Armagnac brandy, as well as to the more conventional Cognac. In the latter region the grape is known as the Folle-Blanche, but appears to be indistinguishable from Picpoul. The 11.5° white wine it makes is rather hard, but the unusual flavour gives it interest.

Our route now takes in, farther to the south-west, the *département* of the Aude, the link between the southern edge of the Massif Central and the eastern side of the Pyrenees. It produces one particular *appellation contrôlée* wine which, for this part of the world, is of exceptional merit — *Blanquette-de-Limoux* — whose reputation as a sparkling wine tends to obscure the very considerable virtues of *Limoux-nature*, the still version. This rather sweet sparkling wine is made by the Champagne method and must have a minimum of 10° of alcohol. Enthusiasts compare it with Champagne, but this comparison cannot be upheld. Certainly it is one of the better local sparkling wines, but compared with the best, the flavour is coarse. The name comes from the grape which is used to the greatest extent in its production, Mauzac. It is interesting to watch the Limoux vineyards when the wind is blowing. The Mauzac leaves disclose their undersides, which are quite white against the green of the leaf tops, and this whiteness gives the wine its name of *blanquette*. Limoux-nature is a drier, very light still wine to which the Mauzac gives an unusual flavour.

There is only one other *A.C.* in this *département*, accorded to the red wines of *Fitou*. These wines are a very deep, ruby red. To attain this colour they must, by the terms of the *A.C.*, be kept at least nine months before being sold. They are quite powerful (12°), soft and pleasant, and among the best wines of a not very promising area.

The *V.D.Q.S.* wines cover a wide range. They are the *Corbières* which are unpretentious, light, of agreeable flavour, and refreshing in the great heat which is normal to this region. The plain Corbières come as red, rosé, and white (11°). The *Corbières-supérieures* are produced from a mixture of better grapes, and are a little stronger (12°). The *Corbières-du-Roussillon* (11°) are produced farther inland from a different range of grapes, and therefore have a different flavour. But I think the best are the *Corbières-supérieures-du-Roussillon* (reds 12°, rosés and whites 12.5^O). These are really very good drinking for this part of France.

For the end of the route we pass into the last *département* in France going westwards along the Mediterranean, the Pyrénées-Orientales, where the production is geared to aperitif and dessert rather than table wines.

There is an *A.C. Grand-Roussillon,* a generic name for the dessert and table wines of the great Roussillon plain. It covers the wines of the *Côtes-d'Agly, Côtes-du-Haut-Roussillon, Maury,* and *Rivesaltes,* all of which produce "natural sweet" and fortified dessert wines, and the differences between them are very difficult to detect. Two producers of similar wines do not come under this generic *A.C.,* but each has one of its own: *Banyuls* and *Frontignan.* The latter wines are also known as *Muscat-de-Frontignan* and *Vin-de-Frontignan.*

These muscatel-type wines are all basically similar, and either one likes them all or one likes none of them. If it is any help to travellers in these parts, my own order of preference would be: Banyuls for consistent quality and excellence; Frontignan for occasional brilliance but perhaps generally less consistent quality; and third, but only just behind Frontignan, the wines of Rivesaltes.

Lastly, if you would like a pleasant "little wine" I recommend the mountain-born *Roussillon-dels-Aspres:* I prefer the white, the rosé, and the red in that order.

Route IV: _____

A Route down the Rhône from Burgundy to the Mediterranean

This is a real wine route to the South, and Chalon-sur-Saône, with its easy access from the north of France or from Switzerland, makes a good starting-point for it. Dijon and the Côte-d'Or and what one can think of as the real Burgundies, the northern ones, are dealt with in a separate chapter, for the area is too rich in great wines and lesser wines for it to be adequately dealt with in the course of a rambling journey.

Beginning as this route does in the *département* of Saône-et-Loire, we start off with the wines of the Beaujolais. But are Beaujolais wines not Burgundies? Historically and geographically Beaujolais was never an integral part of Burgundy. Nor, until quite recent years, were the wines thought of as Burgundies. I quote from the authoritative *Chambers's Encyclopedia* of around 1912: "Beaujolais, a subdivision of the old province of Lyonnais, France, which now forms the northern part of the *département* of the Rhône, and a small part of Loire. Its fine vineyards yield a wine called *Beaujolais,* of which large quantities are exported. It formed at first a separate barony, came into the hands of the Bourbons in 1400, was afterwards united to the crown by Francis I, and next passed into the hands of a nephew of the Constable de Bourbon. It came by marriage to the House of Orleans in 1826, with whom it remained until the Revolution". No word of any union with Burgundy.

Burgundy never stretched beyond Mâcon to the south, where the Beaujolais area may be said to begin. When and how did the wines come to be accepted as Burgundies, so that an eminent expert could write quite recently, "Wines of this type come from the *Mâcon* and *Beaujolais* areas of Burgundy"? So far as this book is concerned a Beaujolais is not a

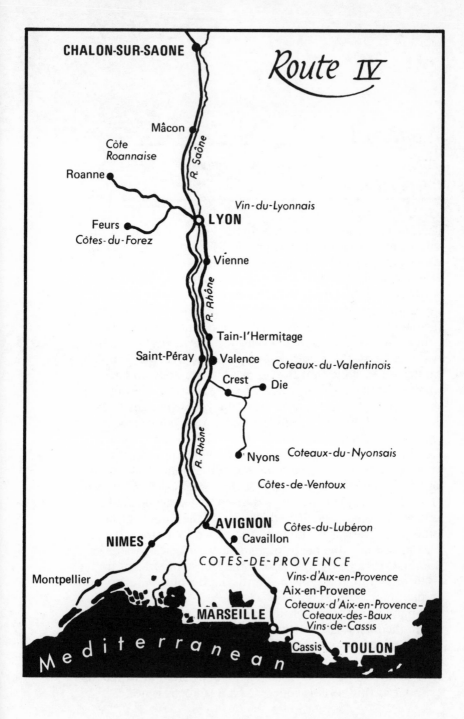

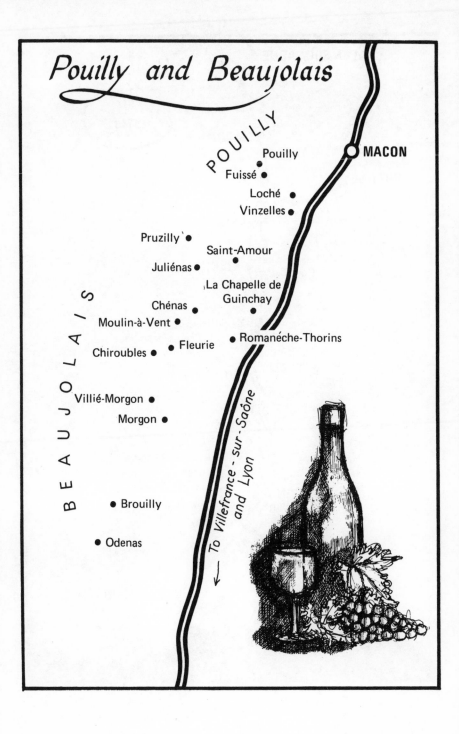

Pouilly and Beaujolais

POUILLY

Pouilly

○ MACON

Fuissé

Loché

Vinzelles

Pruzilly

Saint-Amour

Juliénas

La Chapelle de Guinchay

Chénas

Moulin-à-Vent

Fleurie

Romanéche-Thorins

Chiroubles

Villié-Morgon

Morgon

BEAUJOLAIS

Brouilly

Odenas

To Villefrance - sur - Saône and Lyon

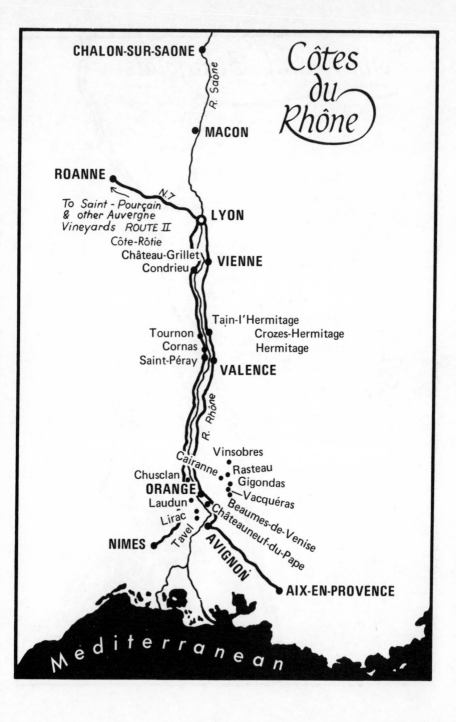

Burgundy. It has not the royal texture, body, and bouquet of the true Burgundies.

It has a generic *A.C.*, *Beaujolais*, of which it is said authoritatively that much more is sold than is ever produced. "Lyons alone", say the French, "consumes each year a quantity of Beaujolais as great as the total production of all the Beaujolais vineyards." What the rest of the wine sold under that name really is can only be guessed at.

Plain Beaujolais is a not very highly coloured red wine, fairly light in body, with a not too pronounced bouquet. It is very refreshing to drink. With certain exceptions noted later, it is a wine to be drunk young, say from twelve to eighteen months to the end of its second year, after which it will probably lose its greatest attraction, its freshness.

Under this same *appellation* come two better versions, *Beaujolais-supérieur* and *Beaujolais-Villages*. There are both white and rosé versions of the various Beaujolais wines, but they are not easy to find, and when they are found they are not as good as the red. So we will consider only the red. The ordinary Beaujolais runs only to 9° of alcohol content. Both the better ones have a minimum of 10°. The difference between them is that Beaujolais-Villages, or "Beaujolais" followed by the name of a specific village, guarantees that the vineyards are within a precise area. The villages in Saône-et-Loire which may give their names to the wines are, for the most part, except Saint-Amour, beneath the best which, in other *départements*, are entitled to use the *appellation* followed by their own name. They are: *Saint-Amour-Bellevue, Chanes, La Chapelle-de-Guinchay, Leynes, Pruzilly, Romanèche, Saint-Symphorien-d'Ancelles,* and *Saint-Vérand*.

There, for a while, we will leave Beaujolais wines to turn to other good wines from this *département*: there are four of them, each with its own *A.C.*, beginning with the three white *Pouilly*. These delicious three are the popular *Pouilly-Fuissé* and the less well-known but still highly meritorious *Pouilly-Vinzelles* and *Pouilly-Loché*. These are 11° wines, unless the generic name is followed by that of a particular locality within the area, in which case the minimum is raised to 12°. They are beautifully flavoured, dry yet soft, made exclusively from the fine Chardonnay grape. They are popular; too popular, for the demand (as with Beaujolais) outruns the supply and the wine in the bottle does not always correspond to the name on the label.

The red wines of *Saint-Amour* are an improved version of most Beaujolais wines. Here again, if the generic title of Saint-Amour is followed by the name of a locality within the area, the alcohol content must have been increased from 10° to 11°. Two other white wines close the list for this area: the sound, well-flavoured wines of *Montagny* and *Givry* (both 11°) rival the whites of the Côte-d'Or but, not having the same reputation, are much less expensive. Montagny only makes white wines, but Givry makes an excellent red as well, quite properly comparable to the excellent white.

Here the *département* of Saône-et-Loire comes to an end and the *département* of the Rhône begins, though, despite its name, this great river only enters it at Lyons, at its southern end. A *V.D.Q.S.* wine, in 9° red and rosé and 9.5^O white versions, grows around Lyons, but is not outstanding in any way. I sometimes wonder who drinks it, seeing the devotion of the good people of Lyons to Beaujolais. "Three rivers", they say, "flow through our city; the Saône, the Rhône, and the Beaujolais. The first two have bridges over them. The last one has no bridge over it and though it flows into the city it never flows out again." So who drinks the *vin du Lyonnais* remains a little mysterious. The Lyonnais will also warn you that their city alone drinks all the Beaujolais that is made. The great unanswered question is, what is the rest?

In the *département* of the Rhône we find not only Beaujolais, Beaujolais-Supérieur, and Beaujolais-Villages again, but also the better part of another thirty *villages*, each with its own named wine. It is hopeless to attempt to distinguish between them individually, but for the record here they are: *Arbuissonnais, Beaujeu, Blacé, Cercié, Charentay, Chénas, Chiroubles, Durette, Emeringes, Fleurie, Juliénas, Jullié, Lancié, Lantigné, Le Perréon, Montmélas, Odenas, Quincié, Regnié, Rivolet, Saint-Etienne-des-Ouillères, Saint-Etienne-la-Varenne, Saint-Julié, Saint-Lager, Salles, Vaux, Villé-Morgon.*

Which to choose of these good, reliable wines? Possibly the best known are Chénas, Chiroubles, Fleurie, and Juliénas, each

of which also has its own *appellation contrôlée.*Other *A.C.*
wines are *Brouilly*, 10° red, and *Côtes-de-Brouilly,* 10.5°
(or 11° if this name is followed by that of a locality, or the
words *Premier Cru).* These again are wines of better flavour
and higher quality than the ordinary Beaujolais.

In this *département* wines labelled "Beaujolais" have a
direct competitor in those labelled "Côtes-du-Rhône". In
addition to those which come under this generic label there
are other lesser ones which, as is the case with the Ardèche
wines, add the name of the *département* to the generic base,
Côtes-du-Rhône-Rhône, as is explained in Route III. There
are also some very, very good wines which benefit by their
own individual *appellation contrôlée.*

The Côtes-du-Rhône vineyards follow each other for well
over a hundred miles along the banks of the great river.
Thirteen principal grapes are allowed within the regulations of
the *A.C.*, and ten secondary ones. Of course these are not all
used at the same time, but the choice enables producers to
vary the grape content according to the very great changes
in soil and climate which are to be expected over this distance.
This is not true of the Beaujolais wines, which are limited to
a Gamay and two Pinots.

Condrieu wines rate the first individual *A.C.* in the *département* among the whites; they are made only from the one
grape, the Voignier, and must reach a minimum of 11° of
alcohol. The flavour given by this unusual grape is unique and
splendid. These wines are quite magnificent and produced
only in very small quantities. An individual vineyard at
Condrieu which has its own *A.C.* is the *Château-Grillet,* a
particularly beautiful version of a Condrieu wine.

Its counterpart in the reds is the admirable *Côte-Rôtie
(A.C.),* surely the very best of the Côtes-du-Rhône reds,
whose soil and situation is such that nowhere else does the
Syrah grape, from which so many other good reds are produced, flourish so well or develop so good a flavour (strength:
10°).

Two outstanding and very popular Beaujolais wines coming
from this area are *Moulin-à-Vent* and *Morgon.*These are also
10° red wines; in both cases, if the *A.C.* name is followed by
a vineyard or village name, the alcoholic strength will be 11°.

They are full-bodied reds of fine flavour, made from one grape, the black Gamay, which gives a purer white juice than most and whose use is called for by the wording of the *appellation contrôlée*.

Alongside the *département* of the Rhône, to the west, is that of the Loire, which by comparison has only a very small production of wine. Red and rosé wines come from near the edge of the Massif Central in the form of *V.D.Q.S. Côtes-du-Forez* and *V.D.Q.S. Côte-Roannaise* (also known as *Vin-de-Renaison*). Though both are made from good Gamay grapes, the degree of alcohol is low at 9° and disappointingly both remain no more than drinkable but dull table wines.

Turning now to the east from the southern end of the *département* of the Rhône we have, across the Rhône on its left bank, the *département* of the Drôme, in which one finds an *A.C.* white wine made from the Clairette grape. It is by no means the best wine produced in this *département*, but a delightful, cheerful little sparkling wine to help make and keep the traveller happy. It is perhaps a pleasing one to start with: *Clairette-de-Die* (10°), available either as a white or as a rosé. It is not a wine to keep as, it is said, it has a tendency to lose some of its sparkle as it gets older. As nobody ever seems even to try to keep it, one wonders how this was ever found out! The rosé is one of the best of its kind I have ever tasted. I have always thought that pink Champagne was rather a waste of the lovely white Champagne it might have been if the red wine had never been mixed with the white, but I am content at any time to take the pink Clairette instead of the white, though curiously the *appellation con-trôlée* covers only the white, not the rosé.

It is when we come to the reds and the whites that the *département* comes into its own, for they are the famous *Hermitage* and *Crozes-Hermitage* of great flavour and good body. These beautiful wines, made solely from the Syrah grape, are not alone, for though most people think of Hermitage *A.C.* wines as red there is also a smaller production of equally beautiful whites (both are produced from the Syrah grape and both carry a minimum 10° of alcohol). Then totally unexpectedly one finds a third Hermitage wine (but not a Crozes-Hermitage), a *vin de paille* comparable with the

Jura wines described in Route V. This is made by gathering
the grapes as late as possible, then laying them on beds of
straw through at least the early part of the winter, and only
then pressing them. It makes a wine of a deep yellow and a
flavour which is quite out of this world. If today there is
still a nectar, this must be it. It will age beautifully, and
improve through the gradual loss of some of its high alcohol
content (14°).

Lastly, there are some sound local wines, varying in quality
but in general worthy ones. They begin with the red, rosé,
and white *V.D.Q.S.* wines of *Châtillon-en-Diois* (10° reds,
10.5^O whites and rosés), pleasantly flavoured from good
grapes, usually inexpensive and a good buy when they are.
Also a *V.D.Q.S.* is the *Haut-Comtat*, red and rosé (11°),
rather strong in flavour, but quite pleasing to drink.

Then come the more ordinary products: *Coteaux-de-la-
Drôme,* red and white; *Coteaux-du-Tricastin,* red; *Coteaux-
du-Nyonsais,* red and white; *Coteaux-du-Valentinois,* red and
white. These are all quite pleasant little wines, of no great
refinement, but none the less more delicate in flavour than
one would, perhaps, have expected.

After this expedition away from the Rhône into the not
very well-known hinterland of the Drôme, the journey down
the river is resumed and leads to the *département* of the
Vaucluse and Roman France. And here we meet the last of
the Côtes-du-Rhône wines, though they are always known
by their own individual *appellation contrôlée, Châteauneuf-
du-Pape.* Both reds and whites are very powerful wines, with
a minimum alcohol content of 12.5^O. The Syrah grape and
the highly flavoured Grenache are the most important con-
stituents of the wines, but individual producers are given a
wide choice, and can ring the changes to a very considerable
extent, so the wines vary in flavour more than is usual with
A.C. wines. They naturally age well but, alas, like so many
other French wines today they are drunk too young in their
country of origin. However, it is perhaps some consolation
that this probably matters less with Châteauneuf-du-Pape
than with some others, for they change comparatively little
in flavour as they age. The white wines seem to be much
less well known than the reds, but none the less they ar3

less well known than the reds, but none the less they are excellent in flavour – and very strong.

Two other *appellation contrôlée* wines are very sweet ones. They are not quite comparable, for the *Muscat-de-Beaumes-de-Venise* (a delightful name which I am sure helps to increase sales) is a wine which tastes very strongly of muscatel, while *Rasteau* tastes of the Grenache grape. The former is made almost entirely of the Muscat-de-Frontignan grape, a very tiny, very sweet one. Both wines have a minimum of 15° alcohol content in their "natural" sweet wine version, that is to say, lightly fortified wines. They both have a *vin de liqueur,* fortified to have a minimum of 22° of alcohol. Apart from the flavour of the respective grapes, the major difference between them is that the Rasteau but not the Muscat can come as a red, a white, a rosé, and a *rancio.*

There are two *V.D.Q.S.* wines, the *Côtes-du-Lubéron* and the *Côtes-du-Ventoux.* They are both rather pallid versions of the Côtes-du-Rhône, less well flavoured and less strong. Though some white and rosé wines are made in both cases, the reds are the best. In a countryside so rich in vineyards, there is an enormous choice of *vins ordinaires,* reasonably good to drink, but with considerable differences in quality according to the year's weather.

Finally we reach the *Bouches-du-Rhône* wines, two of which have their own *appellations contrôlées.* These are *Palette* and *Cassis.* The Palette reds can be made from a wide selection of grapes, but the Grenache is the principal one. Its alcoholic content is 10.5^O. The rosés run to 11° and the whites, produced mainly from Clairette grapes, 11.5^O. The red, white, and rosé wines of Cassis have a much greater reputation. They are all 11° wines, and the white is the favourite. These are all hard, fresh wines which would not be as well considered in an area of greater wines as they are in this *département* on the Mediterranean shore.

The wines of Cassis, and the place itself, have no connection with the *cassis* of *vermouth-cassis,* the classical French aperitif of times gone by, now to a great extent replaced by *vin blanc cassis.* This cassis is blackcurrant cordial, almost invariably made in Dijon.

There are three *V.D.Q.S.* wines in the Bouches-du-Rhône.

These are the *Coteaux-d'Aix-en-Provence*, red, rosé, and white, the first two produced mainly from the Grenache grape (11°) and the white largely on the Clairette (11.5^O). They are also found as *Coteaux-d'Aix-en-Provence-Coteaux-des-Baux,* and as *Coteaux-des-Baux* by itself. The third one is the *Côtes-de-Provence* which continues into two other *départements,* Alpes-Maritimes and Var. These also are red, rosé, and white, and are very similar in the use of grapes and identical in alcohol. They are all hard little wines, these, but not at all unpleasant to drink.

The list, and the journey, closes with three *vins de pays,* rough, drinkable at the right time, but not to be asked for in de luxe hotels: the *Coteaux-du-Roi-René,* the *Coteaux-de-Sainte-Baume,* and the *Coteaux-de-Sainte-Victoire.*

Route V: _____

A Route from the Belgian Frontier through the Vosges, Jura, and Alps to the Côte-d'Azur

This route is a spectacular one visually, but on the wine-tasting side is very mixed. There is almost a preponderance of *vin de pays*, to balance which there are also the very magnificent wines of the Jura and some delicious Alpine wines of less distinction. It is a route primarily through mountains, though it starts off on a pancake-flat plain. Its beginning is at Mézières, near the Belgian frontier. From inside France it is best reached via the Champagne area (for which there is a separate chapter), which gives the opportunity to sample on the way the amiable little *A.C. Rosé-des-Riceys* in the *département* of the Aube. The *département* of the Meuse can be skipped by those joining the route from inside France without any great loss; for them it can more usefully be joined farther south, in Lorraine. However, for those coming in from Belgium, there are some local wines in the Meuse which I have drunk but dare not really praise: the red and *gris* wines of *Buxières, Ecurey, Lissey,* and *Saint-Maurice.* In Lorraine (*département* of Meurthe-et-Moselle) there is not much choice. There is a *V.D.Q.S. Vin-de-la-Moselle* in red and white; in both forms it is a weak wine (only 8.5° of alcohol), made from a great variety of grapes which include the Alsatian Sylvaner and Gamay (both 30 per cent of the total). Another *V.D.Q.S.* is the *Côtes-de-Toul,* again only 8.5° of alcohol, whether it be the white, the rosé, or the red, and produced mainly from Pinot grapes. This wine is adequate but not memorable.

Fortunately Alsace is alongside, and everywhere in Lorraine there is good Alsatian wine to be bought. Owing to the peculiarities of their labelling, the wines of Alsace are dealt with in a separate chapter.

The *département* of the Vosges, with its round-topped hills

over which man and Nature between them have flung carpets
of dark-green pines, is more famous for its landscapes than
its wines. I can remember only two: a red *Epinal* and a white
Neufchâteau, neither very exciting. The same can be said of
the two wines of the Haute-Saône, the reds of *Ray-sur-Saône*
and *Gy,* both a little on the thin side.

Once the *département* of the Doubs is reached the wines
improve and herald the treats yet in store. The whites of
Jalleranges, Buffard, Besançon, and *Vuillafans* are nicely
flavoured, honest *vins-de-pays,* and *Liesle* has a red version as
well as a white.

Then one reaches, joyfully, the *département* of the Jura,
where some of France's most distinguished and least-known
wines are to be met. Quantities grown are small and only
adequate for local consumption. The inhabitants can see no
point in sending them elsewhere. Even when one is there, it
is rare to be able to buy the best, which producers keep for
themselves. Nevertheless, even if the best are not available to
the passer-by, very good ones can be obtained.

To begin with there are the beautiful *A.C.* wines of *Arbois.*
There is a great range of them: red, rosé, and *gris,* produced
largely from the Poulsard or Ploussard grape. This grape gives
the reds a strange pale colour, from whence derives their
quite unofficial name of *pelure-d'oignon,* "onion skin". It is
as unusual in flavour as it is in colour. The whites are more
interesting. They carry a 10.5° alcohol content as compared
with the 10° of the reds. They are produced from Savagnin,
Chardonnay, and Pinot grapes. This *vin blanc* is the earliest
of the three different versions of white wine to be harvested.
Some of the grapes are left to ripen much further before
being crushed. Their fermented juice gives a wine of a deep-
yellow colour: this is the powerful 11.5° *vin jaune* of exqui-
site flavour. The third variation is obtained by letting fully
ripened grapes from the late vintage lie on a bed of straw in
warm, well-ventilated premises until February or even March
before being brought to the wine presses. Though they retain
but little juice, what little there is turns into a marvellous
wine which will go on improving with age to an extraordinary
extent, helpful by its very great 18° alcoholic strength. Inevitably it is expensive; inevitably it is comparatively rare. It is

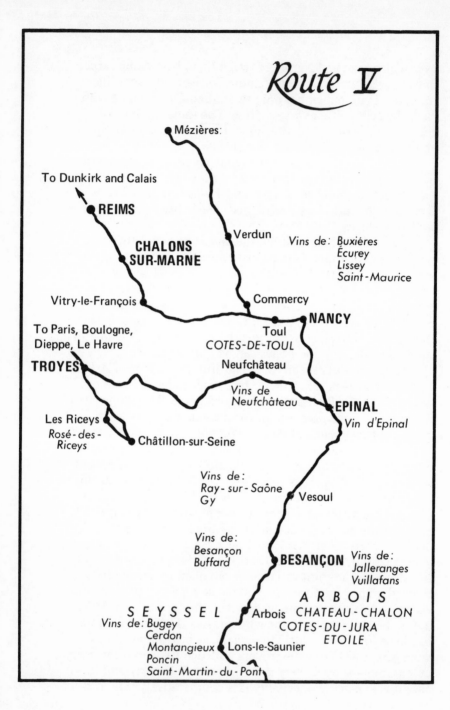

Route V

Mézières:

To Dunkirk and Calais

REIMS

CHALONS
SUR-MARNE

Verdun

Vins de: Buxiéres
Écurey
Lissey
Saint-Maurice

Vitry-le-François

Commercy

NANCY

To Paris, Boulogne,
Dieppe, Le Havre

Toul
COTES-DE-TOUL

TROYES

Neufchâteau

Vins de
Neufchâteau

EPINAL

Vin d'Epinal

Les Riceys

Rosé-des-
Riceys

Châtillon-sur-Seine

Vins de:
Ray-sur-Saône
Gy

Vesoul

Vins de:
Besançon
Buffard

BESANÇON

Vins de:
Jalleranges
Vuillafans

ARBOIS

SEYSSEL

Vins de: Bugey
Cerdon
Montangieux
Poncin
Saint-Martin-du-Pont

Arbois

CHATEAU-CHALON
COTES-DU-JURA
ETOILE

Lons-le-Saunier

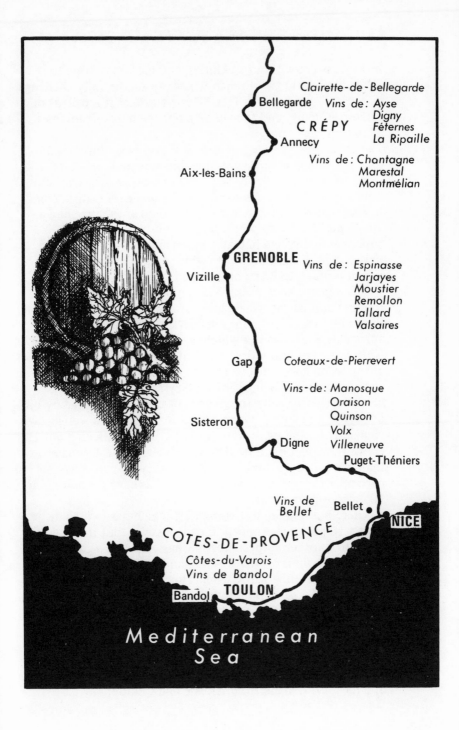

Clairette-de-Bellegarde

Bellegarde

Vins de: Ayse
Digny
Féternes
La Ripaille

CRÉPY

Annecy

Vins de: Chantagne
Marestal
Montmélian

Aix-les-Bains

GRENOBLE

Vins de: Espinasse
Jarjayes
Moustier
Remollon
Tallard
Valsaires

Vizille

Gap

Coteaux-de-Pierrevert

Vins-de: Manosque
Oraison
Quinson
Volx
Villeneuve

Sisteron

Digne

Puget-Théniers

Vins de
Bellet

Bellet

NICE

COTES-DE-PROVENCE

Côtes-du-Varois
Vins de Bandol

Bandol

TOULON

Mediterranean
Sea

mellow, sweet without sickliness, and has a tiny sting to it. Of its kind, only two French wines can successfully challenge it, the *A.C. vin de paille* (the "straw wine" as it is called) of *Château-Chalon*, and the *vin de paille* we have already met at Hermitage.

The plain white wine of *Arbois* is also made into a sparkling one, which is very agreeable, but not supreme in its class. Apart from these two, there are two other *A.C.* wines to note — the *Côtes-du-Jura* and the *Vin-de-l'Etoile*. Both come in four versions, first as a *vin blanc,* then a *vin jaune* and a *vin de paille,* all very good, but not quite of the same supreme quality as Château-Chalon and Arbois. Both also have a gently sparkling white wine of excellent flavour which is much to be recommended.

The *département* of the Ain can be considered either as the first approach to the Alpine area or the last extension of Burgundy. It has only one *appellation contrôlée* wine, the admirable white *Seyssel* which is to be found all through Savoy. Not sweet, not aridly dry, pleasant in flavour and ageing nicely when given the chance, it has many virtues. I shall always remember being shown a Seyssel snowfield in the height of winter, with the surface of the snow marked by bits of twig in a regular pattern. This, I learned, was a well-known vineyard and the twigs were the tops of vines sticking out above three feet of snow. The vine is a great deal tougher than many people think. The Roussette grape gives Seyssel its particular flavour, and the wine is sold as having a minimum 10° alcoholic content.

There is also a *Seyssel mousseux,* which has to include at least a 10 per cent proportion of Roussette, but the bulk is made from other grapes, mostly Chasselas. It is a great favourite at winter-sports resorts, and is a good but not a top-grade sparkling white wine. Then, at *V.D.Q.S.* level come two kinds of *Vin de Bugey,* not the equal of Seyssel, but pleasant, modest wines sold at reasonable prices. The 9.5^{o} Vin de Bugey red or rosé is made from Gamay, Pinot, or Poulsard grapes, or all three, and the corresponding white wine mainly from Chardonnay. The *Roussette de Bugey,* which reaches 10.5^{o} minimum, or 11° if followed by the name of a locality, is made from Altesse and Chardonnay grapes, and is unpretentious but most agreeable to drink. There are even more modest local wines which I have drunk and enjoyed. Four of them I particularly remember: *Saint-Martin-du-Pont, Montangieu, Poncin,* and *Cerdon.* They come in red as well as white editions, but to my mind the white mountain wines are always better than the red. As we enter Haute-Savoie we come to the tall mountains and to the Savoy wines from the deep valleys. The only *A.C.* is *Crépy,* a delicious white wine with a degree of refreshing acidity and good and uniform quality. This 9.5° wine is made from the Chasselas grape, which enters into some of the less considered Alsatian wines, but it seems in this case to produce an altogether better one. The vineyards are productive and a fair quantity is produced. I asked a local producer once why it was seldom or never to be found outside Savoy, and for once a silly question produced a very sensible answer. "What would Monsieur have us do," he asked, "sell all our beautiful wine to other people so that we should be reduced to drinking cheap Italian or Spanish wines ourselves?"

I cannot trace a red wine local to Haute-Savoie, but there are many very pleasing white *vins de pays.*Who could resist the chance of drinking a wine called *La Ripaille,* which means "the beanfeast" though here it is the name of a locality? *Ayse, Digny,* and *Féternes* all produce their white wines, but they are more easily to be found in the taverns and village wine shops than in the hotels and restaurants which specialize in Crépy and Seyssel. The latter, let it be remarked in passing, has some of its vineyards actually in this *département* as well as in the *département* of the Ain.

Savoie follows on Haute-Savoie. Its production is almost entirely of *vins de pays,* with the exception of one *V.D.Q.S.,* the *Vin de Savoie,* which can in fact come from localities in both *départements.* There are white wines, there are *clairet* wines, there are rosé wines, there are *Roussettes,* and there is a *Mousseux de Savoie.* They are all made from a wide assortment of grapes. They are acceptable, but it is difficult to become enthusiastic about them. *Vins de pays* of some local reputation are the reds of *Montmélian* and *Chantagne,* and the whites of *Chantagne* and *Marestal* (this last one I think is the best of them).

Next to Savoie, southwards, are the Hautes-Alpes, a region much less sophisticated than the two *départements* of Savoy. There are no *A.C.* wines, and not even *V.D.Q.S.* ones. Here you are forced to the *vin de pays* level if you wish to drink local products. The whites are of reasonably good flavour but a little thin: *Jarjayes, Moustier, Espinasse, Remollon, Tallard,* and *Valsaires* is a fairly complete list of them, with not much to choose between them.

Surprisingly, in view of this route's swift approach to the fleshpots of the Riviera, the next *département* southwards, the Basses-Alpes, is also delightfully unsophisticated for most of its area. There is one *V.D.Q.S.* wine, *Coteaux de Pierrevert,* white, rosé, and red, quite strong (11° for the red wines, 11.5^O for the others), with the Grenache grape being the principal one used, a sure sign of how far south we have travelled. For the rest there are no others than *vins de pays* of a bucolic nature, with names known only to locals: *Oraison,Quinson, Volx,* and *Villeneuve,* and one more familiar one, *Manosque,* the home town of the late Jean Giono. All these are white wines.

Then comes the last southwards move to the *département* of the Alpes-Maritimes and down to the eye-delighting landscapes and seascapes of the French Riviera and to some new wines, much more sophisticated than those of the Basses-Alpes.

The best known are probably the red, rosé, and white wines of *Bellet,* which have their own *A.C.* They are of good body (11° for the whites, 10.5^O for the reds and rosés), and highly flavoured. The vineyards are of easy access from Nice. Then there are *V.D.Q.S. Côtes de Provence,* which also grow in the nearby *départements* of Var and Bouches-du-Rhône. These are quite powerful wines, the whites having a minimum content of 11.5^O and the reds and rosés 11°. The whites, largely produced from Muscat grapes, are sweet; the reds come from a long list of permitted grapes, chief among which is the Grenache one has learned to expect from these southern wines. In this case also the wide choice of grape content means a great variation of flavour from producer to producer.

Up the mountain slopes, away from the sea, there are some rather rough but not unpleasant reds and whites. *Carros, Colomars,* and *La Gaude* produce reds; whites, once again the better, come from *Vence* and *Villars*. These seem the best choice from among many *vins de pays*. The route leaves the Alpes-Maritimes to find its end in the *département* of the Var. The lovers' greeting which comes with journey's end can be celebrated with the last of the *appellations contrôlées* of these routes, covering the *Bandol* red, rosé, and white wines. They all rate 11° of alcohol. The whites are strongly reminiscent of those of Cassis, less than twenty miles away. The red and rosé are full-bodied and of strong flavour. As we have seen, the Var produces its own versions of the *V.D.Q.S.* Côtes de Provence wines. And if, at your journey's present end, economy has begun to be your watchword, there always remains a *vin de pays*, the red *Côtes du Varois,* which, if you haven't expected too much of it, you should find more than just drinkable.

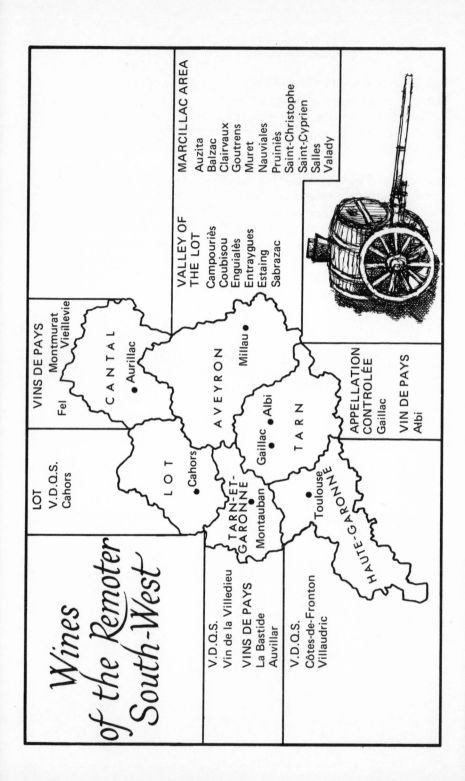

Wines of the Remoter South-West

LOT
V.D.Q.S.
Cahors

VINS DE PAYS
Montmurat
Fel Vieillevie

VALLEY OF THE LOT
Campouriès
Coubisou
Enguialès
Entraygues
Estaing
Sabrazac

MARCILLAC AREA
Auzita
Balzac
Clairvaux
Goutrens
Muret
Nauviales
Pruiniès
Saint-Christophe
Saint-Cyprien
Salles
Valady

APPELLATION CONTROLÉE
Gaillac

VIN DE PAYS
Albi

V.D.Q.S.
Vin de la Villedieu

VINS DE PAYS
La Bastide
Auvillar

V.D.Q.S.
Côtes-de-Fronton
Villaudric

CANTAL
● Aurillac

LOT
● Cahors

AVEYRON
● Millau

TARN
Gaillac ● ● Albi

TARN-ET-GARONNE
● Montauban

HAUTE-GARONNE
● Toulouse

Wines in the Remoter South-west

There is a little group of south-western *départements*, running from the edge of the Massif Central to the central Pyrenees, which it was not possible to fit conviently into the five "wine routes", though some of the wines grown in them are interesting and deserve their mention. Even if others are only *vins de pays* they should not be entirely omitted.

Aveyron

(a) There are some quite interesting *vins de pays* produced in the valley of the river Lot in the villages of *Estaign, Coubisou, Sabrazac, Entraygues, Campouriès*, and *Enguialès*. They are all red wines.

(b) Others, also reds, come from the area around *Marcillac*, including the villages of *Auzita, Balzac, Clairvaux, Goutrens, Muret, Nauviales, Pruiniès, Saint-Cyprien, Saint-Christophe, Salles*, and *Valady*.

Cantal

Red and white wines from *Fel* (known for many centuries), *Montmurat*, and *Vieillevie*.

Haute-Garonne

Two *V.D.Q.S.* wines, both made in red, rosé, and white versions, labelled *Côtes-de-Fronton* and *Villaudric*.

Lot

The *V.D.Q.S.* wine of *Cahors*. This red wine was famous in England all through the Middle Ages. Little is left of the vineyards after the ravages of phylloxera, but the vine has been and still is being gradually replanted, the wine is improving, and more vineyards will surely follow.

Tarn

The white wines of *Gaillac* merit their own *appellation con-trôlée*. They range from sweet to very sweet, the latter usually being sold as *Gaillac doux*. Both versions have an alcohol content of 10.5°. The traditional *Sémillon, Sauvignon,* and *Muscadelle* grapes which produce the *Sauternes* of the Bordeaux area enter into this product, though not necessarily alone, as is the case in Bordeaux. There is also a very powerful 12° *Gaillac-Premières-Côtes*. Both versions are made into a sparkling wine.
A pleasant little *vin de pays,* white, comes from *Albi* and another from *Lavour*.

Tarn-et-Garonne

The *V.D.Q.S. Vin de Villedieu* comes as a 10.5° red of strong flavour. The sweet 11° white is based on the traditional Sauvignon, Sémillon, and Muscadelle grapes, but with many lesser ones thrown in as well: this also is a wine of strong flavour.

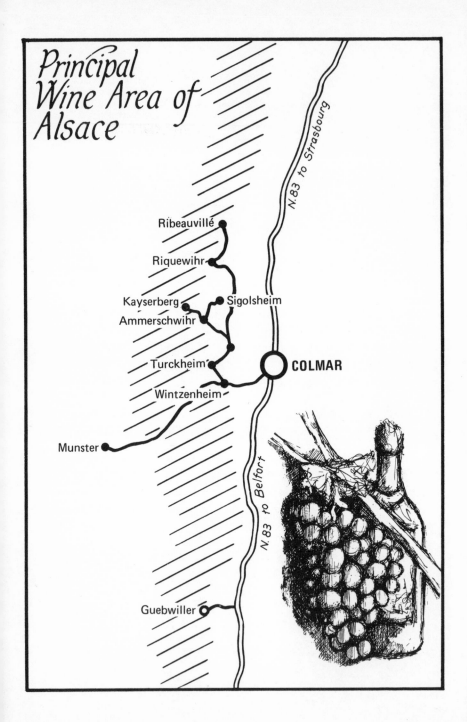

Principal Wine Area of Alsace

Ribeauvillé
Riquewihr
Kayserberg
Ammerschwihr
Sigolsheim
Turckheim
Wintzenheim
Munster
Guebwiller
COLMAR
N.83 to Strasbourg
N.83 to Belfort

Four Great Wine Areas:
Alsace – Champagne – Bordeaux – Burgundy

ALSACE

Alsace is the unofficial but universally accepted term for France's two Rhine-side *départements*. The Rhine here flows from south to north: Bas-Rhin is downstream and northwards, Haut-Rhin is upstream and southwards.

As a wine-growing area Alsace is remarkable as being the only one in France which calls its best wines by the name of the grape from which each one is made, with no geographical distinction other than the name of the entire region. It is usual with French wines that the more general the title, the less good is the wine, and the more limited the area defined by the label, the better the wine should be. Quite clever Frenchmen, usually Parisians, think they are doing well in the course of a holiday journey in Alsace to buy wines which carry the name of a particular village, believing they are getting a better wine than one just carrying the name of a grape, and at what is obviously a bargain price. In fact, unless the label is also clearly marked *Alsace* as its principal title, the exact opposite is the truth, for the only *appellation contrôlée* in Alsace is – *Alsace!*

This *appellation Alsace,* or *Vin d'Alsace,* can only be applied to white wines made from the so-called "noble" grapes: Traminer, Riesling, Pinot, Tokay (in reality, Pinot gris), Clevner, Muscat, and Sylvaner. The wines made from these grapes in alphabetical order are:

Gewürztraminer, a wine of flavour and bouquet peculiar to itself. The *Gewürz* part of it may indicate that the Traminer grapes are very late gathered, after *Botrytis cinerea* has been at work on them, as with the Sauternes and the Monbazillacs. It is a dessert wine of the finest quality, and one which improves in bottle; Traminer is in every way a less distinguished wine.

Muscat, a wine whose name, flavour, and perfume is most readily associated with sweetness, unexpectedly turns out to be a dry one. It is very powerfully flavoured, and perhaps smacks a little more of the soil than other wines coming under the *appellation Alsace.*

Pinot (Pinot blanc), a gentle, dryish wine of good body, less highly flavoured than Muscat and less highly perfumed, but altogether more sophisticated.

Pinot gris is often called *Tokay d'Alsace,* but nobody seems to know why for it is not even remotely connected with the famous Hungarian *Tokay.* Like the Pinot blanc, this wine is less individualistic in flavour and bouquet than some of the other wines made from "noble" grapes, but has more body than they do.

So much for the white wines, but the *appellation* also covers red wines made from Pinot-noir-fin or other Pinot grapes. However, compared with the whites, they are quite indifferent wines. They include the *Clairet-d'Alsace,* a red wine produced from the Pinot grapes already mentioned and the Pinot-meunier in addition. Only its particularly clear colour distinguishes it from the other Alsatian reds. It is also known as *Schillerwein.*

There is a down-grading of the *appellation* allowed for blended wines. If the blends are of different wines made from "noble" grapes only, without any one of them dominating, the wine may be sold as *Alsace Edelzwicker* (this word means "noble mixture"). If the blend is of wines made from "noble" grapes with wines made from second-category grapes (usually Chasselas, Goldreisling, and Knipperlé), then "Alsace" or "Vin d'Alsace" on the label must be followed by the word "Zwicker", which means simply "mixture".

CHAMPAGNE

"The King of wines, the wine of Kings" is not quite how the sixteenth-century chronicler expressed his thought, though it is a fair paraphrase. His own words were that it was "a wine for Kings, Princes and great Nobles". In those days it was probably not a white wine at all but a red which neither kept nor travelled well, and had a natural inclination to bubble again in the spring and complete its unfinished autumn fermentation. By 1668 the area was producing good white wines which lay dormant all through their first winter but came to life after hibernation to sparkle a second time as the spring came slowly to this northern area.

Monasteries played a great part in the production of wine in the province of Champagne. The monastery of Hautvillers in the Marne valley was to the forefront of them all. In 1670 they appointed one Dom Pérignon to be their cellarer. He had already been observing with growing interest the phenomenon of double fermentation, and in this monastery he had the opportunity and the leisure to pursue his inquiries. He experimented with various methods of clarifying white wine, and did excellent pioneer work in this field. His name goes down in history principally as the man who introduced the cork as a stopper for wine bottles, but although he employed this substance he did not originate its use. His example widened its use very substantially. Previously oiled hemp wrapped round a wooden stopper was the method used to shut off the neck of a bottle, but the method was so inefficient that much of the wine turned to vinegar or was otherwise spoiled. It was the cork which did so much to increase the life of other wines. To Champagne it did more; it made the production of sparkling wine possible. Dom Pérignon also seems to have been a pioneer in the transformation of the casual mixing of wines into something approaching the scientific blending of different wines which is the very basis of the Champagne trade today.

The area in which Champagne is produced is remarkably small for so widely sold a product. It represents only about 1 per cent of the vines in France's wine-producing regions. It is situated about 100 miles east-north-east of Paris. It is divided into three parts: La Montagne de Reims, which is no mountain at all, but a low hill in the valley of the river Vesle, facing northwards across the river; next is the Marne valley, near Epernay, facing east; lastly, the Côte-des-Blancs, "the white-grape slopes" to the south-west of Epernay, facing east. The region includes part of the *départements* of the Marne, the Aisne, and the Aube; in the case of the last, it is only much

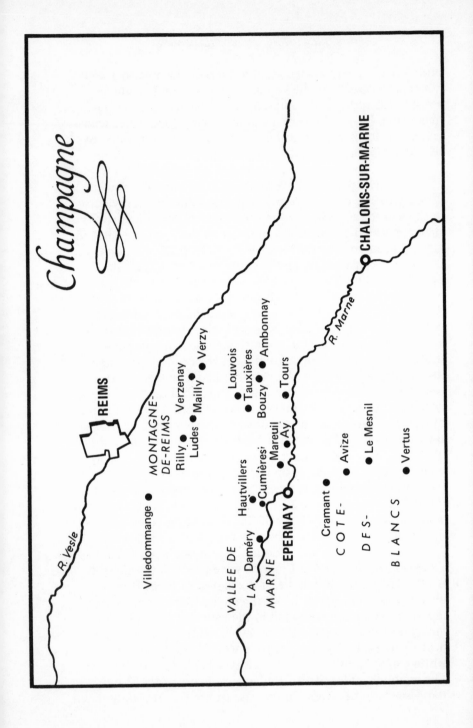

smaller areas near Bar-sur-Aube and Bar-sur-Seine which are
concerned. Until 1790 Champagne was the name of the
province which included the Champagne area.

It is in every way a remarkable region. As the map of the
limits of the vine in France shows, this is the northernmost
area to grow grapes commercially, and some of the vineyards
are right on the imaginary line which marks the limits. On
the face of it, the chalk soil hardly seems a hospitable one and
unlikely to achieve such outstanding results in vine cultivation.
The climate is downright bad, often with cold and wet autumns.
In extreme cases the vintage can be prolonged into November.

Traditional, fine-quality grapes manage to thrive in these
apparently unsatisfactory conditions. Two splendid Pinots
(Pinot noir and Pinot gris) are the mainstay, supported by the
somewhat less esteemed Pinot meunier and Chardonnay, this
last being the only white grape among the four. Some of the
less excellent wines will also include Meslier and Ardanne
grapes, but these are excluded from the best-quality wines.
The Pinots need very careful handling, for the slightest contact
with the skins will risk some reddening of the juice.

The wines from the Côte-des-Blancs are based on the
Chardonnay grape and are sold as *Blanc-de-Blancs,* "white
wine from white grapes". Whether there is a real difference in
flavour which the occasional, unprofessional wine drinker
could detect, I am not sure.

However, all four of these choice grapes share certain
qualities without which Champagne could not be the great
wine it is. They all mature early, they have a high sugar
content, they thrive on chalky soil, they develop stamina
from a poor climate, and they give the wine a delicate bouquet.

The whole process of producing Champagne differs from
normal procedure. When the grapes have been picked they
are carried to the presses on sprung carts, so as to avoid the
consequences of heavy bumping which might release the
undesired, colour-producing tannins. The presses of great
diameter cope with a load of four metric tons of grapes at a
time (this load is called a *marc*). Very gentle pressure is
applied at first, and then increased gradually over the next
one and a half to two hours. This gives juice enough to make
ten casks of must. A *marc* produces in all thirteen casks of

200 litres each. The first ten casks make the *vin de cuvée*. A further squeezing for one and a half hours suffices to fill the remaining three casks with what are called the *tailles,* used for second-quality wines of darker colour and less delicate flavour, though still allowed to be sold under the same *appellation contrôlée.* This is not the case, however, with the subsequent, final squeeze, which gives *vins de suite,* still wines of indifferent quality not allowed a name.

The freshly pressed must goes into fermentation cellars in which the temperature is maintained between 18° and 20^OC. (64.4^O to 68^OF.). When the fermentation ceases the new wine is racked and tucked away after it has been blended and a syrup of cane sugar in Champagne is added to produce the right amount of bubble. It is this supremely careful blending of one wine with another, sometimes of different years, which enables the firms to continue what might be termed their "house flavour" for generation after generation.

The wine is bottled in the spring and sent to underground cellars of immense size dug deep into the chalk where the temperature is constant. Then the miracle happens. Deep below the ground fermentation starts again, a phenomenon not unknown to housewives who make their own strawberry jam. The residual sugar begins to be transformed into carbonic gas. The second fermentation is not impetuous like the first, and the bubbles form slowly. At the same time the wine throws a sediment. As soon as the second fermentation is over away goes the wine to cool cellars, with a low, unchanging temperature of 10^OC. (50^OF.) for a stay of at least a year. Then they are placed in racks, nose down, and the *remuage* begins. For sheer expertise there are few operatives in other industries to compare with the *remueur,* the man who goes round the racks and gives every bottle a slight rotary movement combined with a tiny movement towards the perfectly vertical. It is said an experienced man can turn 30,000 bottles a day. The double movement gives the sediment a slight twist downwards and, though it is as light as gossamer, it is eventually screwed down through the wine to land on the inner end of the cork, now uppermost.

When this has been achieved the *dégorgement* begins. The cork is swiftly drawn and enough froth poured out to ensure

that all the sediment comes with it. The five or six lost centi-
litres are replaced by the *liqueur d'expédition,* a syrup made
from old wine, cane sugar, and a drop or two of brandy dis-
tilled from the wine. This determines the degree of sweetness
of the final product.

Lastly comes the corking and what the French call the
habillage, the "dressing" of the bottle with all its trappings and
fineries. The cork, of course, is all-important and it is amazing
how vague many experienced Champagne drinkers can be
about it. Is it all of one piece, or is it in many pieces? If so,
how many? Those who do know have won many a bet on it.

There are three pieces. The bottom piece, with which the
wine in the bottle will be in contact, must be smooth and
without defect or over the years it might give the wine a taste.
The second is hard cork to cling tightly to the inside of the
neck of the bottle when it is put in under pressure. The third
is the soft cork top which swells out over the top of the bottle
neck under pressure and gives the cork as a whole the typical
Champagne shape.

Even now that is not quite the end of the story. Another
three years pass (less with some of the cheaper wines) before
a bottle of good Champagne is ready to go out into the world.
What a benefactor it is. Women are all the lovelier, their eyes
all the brighter for it. Conversation is easier. The old bore
suddenly becomes amusingly loquacious. Most people are
brighter, happier, and more friendly under its gentle influence;
none are any the worse. If it is not spoiled by being preceded
or followed by spirits, it never causes any regrets. Its flavour
is as clean and bright as the wine itself. Champagne really is a
great benefactor.

Champagne rosé

Sparkling Champagne is essentially a white wine, but some
sparkling rosé is made, as mentioned above. Its colour is
delicate, its taste less good than that of a white. It is unusual
in that its colour comes from mixing red wine with white and
not from the tannin in the skins.

Champagne nature

A generation ago no self-respecting French *gourmet* being

served with oysters at a good restaurant would have thought of drinking anything but still Champagne with them. In more recent years it has become more difficult to find and proportionately much dearer to buy than it used to be. Now it may only be made when there is over-production of grapes beyond the needs of the producers of sparkling Champagne.

Champagne nature also comes as a red and rosé, but these are far less distinguished in flavour than the white, which remains the incomparable wine to take with shellfish.

BORDEAUX

The Bordelais, as the French call the wine-growing area round Bordeaux, is one of the greatest in the world. It is enormous in size, occupying a very large proportion of France's biggest "county", the *département* of the Gironde. Its production of wine is in keeping with its size: it can reach a million gallons a year, and even more in an exceptional year, though it is generally a little below the million mark. A semi-official figure gives the area planted with vines as about 65,000 hectares. The variety of its wines is also immense, ranging from some which must be considered among the world's finest down to some very ordinary ones.

Geographically, the area is dominated by its rivers. Starting from the Pyrenees, the Garonne flows northwards through Bordeaux. A little downstream from the city it joins the Dordogne, which begins life in the Massif Central in the very centre of France. After their junction the common river is known as the Gironde and emerges into the Bay of Biscay.

To take the Gironde first, from its estuary it edges a fairly narrow strip of land called the Médoc, which has the Gironde as a boundary on the east, and the Bay of Biscay on the other side of the peninsula to the west. The eastern bank of the Gironde is the limit first of the Blaye and then of the Bourg vineyards, producing wines which are only doubtfully Bordeaux. South of the junction with the Dordogne, the Garonne has on its right bank the extensive vineyards of Entre-Deux-Mers, to the limits of the area. On the western bank, first of the Gironde, then of the Garonne, the Médoc vineyards are northern neighbours of the Graves, and the

Graves wines give place to the Sauternes and the Barsacs to the southern limit of the area. The banks of the Dordogne and its little tributary, the Isle, harbour the vineyards of Saint-Emilion and Fronsac.

That, in broad outline, is the Bordelais. Now for its individual wines.

Bordeaux and Bordeaux-Supérieur

A label on a bottle of wine sold only as a "Bordeaux", even though it is an *appellation contrôlée* wine, tells you very little about what may be in the bottle. It tells you that the wine was produced from vineyards within the Bordelais, but it only gives you some very vague idea, so enormous is the area. It tells you that a red or rosé wine was made from a choice of six grapes, but it fails to determine the proportions in which each one may be included. All we know precisely is that it must reach a 10° alcohol content. From this it is clear that a great variety in quality and flavour occurs under this *A.C.*

The position is slightly worse for the white wines, which are based on the white Bordeaux trinity of Sémillon, Sauvignon, and Muscadelle; but up to 30 per cent of the juice from four other and lesser grapes may enter into the wine. The white wines are a little stronger, rating 10.5^O. These plain Bordeaux *A.C.* wines nevertheless have one negative virtue; at least as bought in France they are free from disagreeable surprises. This is a virtue not without its value where cheap wines are concerned.

Under the same *appellation* come some improvements on the standard Bordeaux. There is *Bordeaux-Clairet* or *Bordeaux-Rosé* running to not less than 11° of alcohol. There are the white wines of *Bordeaux-Haut-Benauge* with an alcohol content of not less than 11.5^O, and there is a *Bordeaux-Côtes-de-Castillon* red with not less than 11°. These stronger wines are well worth the little extra money they cost. They keep better for the extra alcoholic strength, and they taste better. The *Haut-Benauge* wines can only be made from the three best grapes.

Under a different *appellation* are the wines sold as *Bordeaux-Supérieur*, which are stronger than the plain

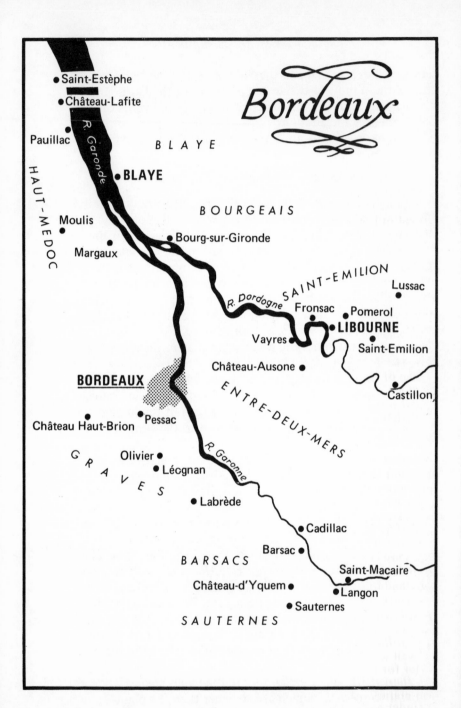

Bordeaux: the reds have 10.5^O and the whites 11.5^O, with a limitation on the grapes which may be used to make the latter.

Improvements on the Bordeaux-Supérieur are denoted by the same names as for Bordeaux. We get *Bordeaux-Supérieur-Clairet* (or *-Rosé*) at 11°, and *Bordeaux-Supérieur-Côtes-de-Castillon* (also 11°).

The Côte-de-Castillon wines come from the far eastern side of Saint-Emilion, and the Haut-Benauge wines from the southeastern end of the Bordeaux vineyards, to the east of the Garonne.

Bordeaux-mousseux

There is a third generic *appellation contrôlée, Bordeaux-mousseux,* white or rosé (final 11°), with again such a wide choice of grapes that no two of these sparkling wines seem to taste the same. For myself, sparkling Bordeaux is an acquired taste which I have not yet succeeded in acquiring: perhaps I have not been persistent enough in my efforts to do so.

Côtes-de-Bordeaux-Saint-Macaire

This *A.C.* covers strong (11.5^O) sweet wines from the extreme south of the area on the right bank of the Garonne. Basically they are from the great trinity of white wine grapes, with very limited adulteration (only up to 10 per cent permitted, with Colombard or Mauzac).

Loupiac and Sainte-Croix-du-Mont

In this same part of the Bordelais are two other *A.C.* wines. *Loupiac* are powerful (13°) white wines, made exclusively from the three quality grapes which make Sauternes, whose vineyards face those of Loupiac across the river. They are not as fine as the Sauternes, but they are none the less wines of some quality. The wines of *Sainte-Croix-du-Mont* are of very high quality. They are white wines similar to but much more refined than those of Loupiac. They too are very strong at 13°.

Premières-Côtes-de-Bordeaux

These vineyards are a continuation downstream, as far as Bordeaux, of those of the *Premières-Côtes-de-Bordeaux-Saint-*

Macaire. They look across the Garonne to the Graves vineyards on the other side of the river. Both sweet and fairly
dry whites are made, the former bearing some likeness to the
Graves of the left bank. The reds are palatable and made from
good grapes, but not to be compared with the Médoc or Saint-
Emilion reds. The reds have an alcohol content of 10.5^O and
the whites of 12°. Two special titles are *Premières-Côtes-de-
Bordeaux-Cadillac* and *Premières-Côtes-de-Bordeaux-Gabarnac,*
the last word in each case being that of a locality of origin.
Both are 11.5^O reds. Whites which end with a name in this
way will have a strength of 13°.

Entre-Deux-Mers

This is a vast area producing sweetish white wines of no
distinction. The alcohol content is not less than 11.5^O, and
the three great white grapes of Bordeaux must make up 70
per cent of the final wine, with lesser grapes used for the
remaining 30 per cent. It seems very strange that the result
is so uninteresting.

Blaye and Côtes-de-Blaye

Like the preceding ones, the wines of Blaye have their own
appellation contrôlée, but it is doubtful if they merit consid-
eration as Bordeaux wines. If they fail to come up to their
own *A.C.* requirements they may not be sold either as
Bordeaux-supérieur, or even as plain Bordeaux. The output
from these vineyards along the right bank of the Gironde,
nearing the estuary, is enormous. The whites are of indifferent
quality; the reds are better, but certainly not in any way outstanding. Both rate 10° of alcohol; both are products of a
big choice of grapes, eight for the whites and seven for the
reds. One seldom sees the name *Blaye* on a bottle. What
happens to this vast output? Blending with others is the
probable answer.

The white *Côtes-de-Blaye* are an improvement; better grapes
and an alcohol content of 11°. Better still are the *Premières-
Côtes-de-Blaye* (a separate *A.C.,* as is the case with the Côtes-
de-Blaye). The 11° whites are made exclusively from the
Sémillon, Sauvignon, and Muscadelle grapes which are the
basis of the very finest Bordeaux whites, and the 10.5^O reds

count two aristocrats (Cabernet Franc and Cabernet Sauvignon) among the four grapes from which this wine may be made.

Bourg (or Côtes-de-Bourg)

Here again is a very large area along the banks of the Gironde and producing very large quantities of not very high quality wines. There is, however, a good deal of variation between the best and the least good. Those sold as *Côtes-de-Bourg* are better than those sold as plain *Bourg*, though its own *A.C.* covers both. The *A.C.* does not cover the red wines of this area, only the 11° whites. If a wine fails the basic requirements of the *A.C.*, like the wines of Blaye it may not be sold as Bordeaux-supérieur but, unlike Blaye, may be sold as Bordeaux.

At this point, the *Bordeaux* picture changes completely. We have finished with the cheap and sometimes indifferent products of the *Bordelais* and enter the realm of the good, the great, and the very great wines, both white and red, which have given the area its world-wide reputation. Where better to start than the northernmost point of the vineyard area, in the Médoc? But before meeting the first of the great wines, one thing must be made clear. There are perhaps in the Bordelais 1,000 growers whose wines are worth keeping and which are named after a château (in many cases the one-time château has long since fallen), and it would be far beyond the scope of this book to give them all. Even the official classification of the *Grands Crus,* the greatest wines of Bordeaux, gives eighty-six names, and as it was prepared in 1855 and a great many changes have taken place since then it seems useless to include that. So by and large individual wines are seldom universally known names, and these that are occupy a top rank.

Médoc

The northernmost point of the Médoc peninsula is Pointe-de-Grave, which is linked to Royan across the wide estuary by a car ferry. Those who land there will find little to interest them for the first twenty miles southwards. This part used to be called Bas-Médoc, and the rest, from near Bordeaux southwards, was (and is still) known as Haut-Médoc. As the people of Bas-Médoc resented the suggestion of inferiority apparent in the name "Low Médoc" they created a great fuss, and the region is now known as just Médoc and Haut-Médoc remains Haut-Médoc. There is a generic *A.C., Médoc,* which includes both parts, and covers 10° red wines. It is not much more than a high-class *vin ordinaire* and varies greatly from producer to producer, but it is often an excellent buy.

Just across the border between Médoc and Haut-Médoc the latter's claim to pride of place begins with the wines of *Saint-Estèphe* – red wines, as are all Médocs, with a very distinctive flavour and a faint suggestion of the good earth which is far from disagreeable. They go on improving with age, far beyond the point at which most wines would be going downhill. All the Médocs are ruby-tinted, as clear as the precious stone itself, and all mellow with the years. With capital locked up during all this time, they are necessarily expensive. But they make most other wines, even very good wines, seem just that little bit coarse after their own highly civilized delicacy.

Next, upstream, are the wines of *Pauillac,* named after the little river port on the edge of the vineyards. And among them are wines which, if you can afford to buy almost regardless of expense, will grace any celebration meal: *Château-Lafite, Château-Latour,* and the magnificent *Château-Mouton-Rothschild.*

It is difficult to find words which will differentiate one great Médoc from another. *Saint-Julien,* next up the river, is obviously a different wine from Pauillac, a shade less masculine, a shade more silky in texture. Its full title is *Saint-Julien-Beycheville.*

At this point we go inland from the river to *Listrac;* the gravelly slopes running down to the Gironde, not far from where it disappears to form the Dordogne and the Garonne, soon make their absence felt. The wines of Listrac are sound and interesting, but they lack the sophistication of those of Pauillac and Saint-Julien. In general terms they are not individual wines but blends from wines made in the area and brought together by the *Co-opérative des Producteurs de*

Listrac. They are good wines, but lack the ultimate *finesse.*
Also well inland from the river is *Moulis-en-Médoc,* a centre
for about a score of pleasing and dependable wines. There is
one exceptional quality with a splendidly eighteenth-century
name — *Château-Chasse-Spleen* — "Away with irritable
gloominess!" This dates from the time when this same irritable
gloominess was supposedly the outstanding characteristic of
the grumpy English.

From there one returns to the river and the gravel slopes
in order to end this summary of Médoc wines on a high note.
Of all the *appellations contrôlées* of the Haut-Médoc there
is non more highly considered than the very delicate and
beautifully scented wines of *Margaux,* of which the most
famous are certainly those of *Château-Margaux.* This must
rank high among the élite of the world's wines.

Graves

The wines of the Haut-Médoc end just north of Bordeaux.
Around this pleasant city the wines of *Graves* flourish. They
are, as the name implies, the products of gravelly soils.

In Britain a majority of wine drinkers think of Graves as
white wines, but the *appellation contrôlée* makes it clear
that there are reds as well. In fact, the *A.C.* covers red 10°,
white 11°, and a 12° *Graves-supérieures,* also white. The red
wines are very good; they made the name of Graves famous
in England long before the whites were heard of, for the whole
area is probably one of Europe's oldest wine-producing centres
and the wines it produced in past centuries were all red. The
still-existing *Château-Ausone* is a reminder that the Roman
poet Ausonius retired to this property of his to spend his old
age caring for the already long-established vineyards.

Of late years there has been a tendency to make the white
Graves a little less sweet than had been the fashion, and ready
to be drunk with satisfaction a little earlier. These consistently
uniform wines are now perhaps undervalued. Of the château-
named Graves, *Château-Haut-Brion* commands the greatest
respect.

Sauternes

Upstream, along the left bank of the Garonne, the gravel soil gives way to a mixture of clay, limestone, and gravel which is ideally suited to that already much referred to triumvirate, Sémillon, Sauvignon, and Muscadelle. Here they are allowed to ripen to their fullest extent until they shrivel up and are acted upon by *Botrytis cinerea,* whose effect is described in Route II in connection with the wines of Monbazillac. For the *Sauternes,* once the scanty but immensely rich juice has been squeezed out in the presses and fermentation has taken place, the resultant wine is hidden away from the world in wooden casks for three years before it is allowed to be bottled. Once in bottle, it will go on improving and developing an ever more satisfying flavour for at least a generation. Much of this lasting quality is due to its high degree of alcohol — a minimum of 13°.

Such wines are necessarily expensive and the best known of them, the wines of *Château-d'Yquem,* command very high prices. There are others, such as *Château-Rieussec,* which are only a little less eminent and quite a lot less expensive. Even the most ordinary of the wines entitled to the Sauternes label are like bottled sunshine, and a glass with the sweet makes a delightful ending to a meal.

Barsac

This *appellation contrôlée* belongs to the wines of a small area on the northern border of the Sauternes region. These sweet wines have, perhaps, less of the highly individual flavour of the Sauternes and are very sweet. It is not the cloying sweetness of some white wines from some other countries. In the North of England I have been offered it to drink all through a meal. The more wine-fashion-conscious southerners who might be inclined to smile at this as an exhibition of northern ignorance should learn from the experience of a friend of mine. A great wine lover, he was asked to join the owners of one of the smaller Barsac vineyards at a family lunch. The main dish was a splendid *gigot,* and with this leg of mutton and the other delicious dishes they all drank the family Barsac.

The Barsacs have nothing quite as regal to offer as Château-d'Yquem, but their own *Château-Coutet* and *Château-Climens* are very distinguished wines. The Barsacs, incidentally,

have their own *A.C.* and are made from the same grapes and
have the same alcohol content as the Sauternes.

Cérons

By the river, at the extreme northern end of this particular
area, stands little Cérons, surrounded by vineyards. Its wine
has its own *A.C.*, is made from the same three grapes, and
has an alcohol content of 12.5°. It is a curious wine, with a
definite flavour of the Graves and an echo of the Barsacs.
There is a considerable variation in sweetness from one
producer to another.

Saint-Emilion

Moving diagonally north-east from Cérons across the Garonne
and on to the right bank of the Dordogne, we come to where
the magnificent wines of *Saint-Emilion* are produced. Are they
as good as, better than, or less good than the Médocs? One
can only reply that they are very different and that it is wrong
to attempt to compare one with the other. The Saint-Emilions
are more robust, and seem to come half-way between the
delicacy of the Médocs and the vigour of the Côtes-de-Beaune.

The *A.C.* of the generic title "Saint-Emilion" calls for an
alcohol content of 11°, but there are increasingly refined
versions, *Saint-Emilion-Grand Cru, Saint-Emilion-Grand-Cru-
Classé* and *Saint-Emilion-Premier-Grand-Cru-Classé,* which
demand a minimum figure of 11.5°. These are all red wines.
The vintage is spread over several stages of selection of the
ripest grapes so that on any one day only grapes that are fully
ready will be picked.

Sables-Saint-Emilion

This is a semi-generic *A.C.* for wines growing mainly between
Saint-Emilion and Libourne, eastwards of the Pomerol wines,
and covers red wines with a minimum alcoholic strength of
10.5°. In addition to the general title there are five sub-
divisions, each referring to wines with a minimum 11° of
alcohol; these are *Lussac-Saint-Emilion, Montagne-Saint-
Emilion* (the *Montagne* is a suburb quite close to Saint-Emilion),
Puissegain-Saint-Emilion, Parsac-Saint-Emilion, and *Saint-
Georges-Saint-Emilion* whose vineyards approach those of

Bordeaux-Côtes-de-Castillon and whose wines, even more perhaps than some of the others, repay some years in bottle; it is only at its best after six years.

Côtes-Canon-Fronsac

The river Isle runs into the Dordogne and in the pocket made by the junction of the two rivers these wines are produced. These 11° reds are fine, rich wines which inevitably bring the Bourgognes to mind even though they are much lighter.

Côtes-de-Fronsac

Wines of the same alcohol content as the Côtes-Canon-Fronsac, but a little less distinguished. Good, sound wines of pleasant flavour none the less.

Pomerol, Lalande-de-Pomerol, and Néac

This trio of wines from north of Libourne have their own joint *appellation*. At 10.5° of alcohol they are a little less strong than some of their neighbours, but are particularly well flavoured and agreeable.

Sainte-Foy-Bordeaux

These wines are closely associated with those of Saint-Emilion, but differ in providing an 11° white wine which is distinguished by its almost excessive sweetness. The 10.5° red has an original flavour very difficult to pin down; perhaps a little of the flavour of a Graves mingling with a stronger one reminiscent of Saint-Emilion. In both cases these are highly individual, but not really distinguished.

Graves-de-Vayres

Geographically these *Graves-de-Vayres* reds and whites (both 10.5°) belong to Saint-Emilion, though they are like none of the other wines from this area. The vineyards occupy gravel slopes on the left bank of the Dordogne, far away from the other Graves slopes on the far side of the Garonne.

The whites are much the same as many of the other semi-sweet table wines of the Bordelais, but the reds are full-bodied, soft-textured wines of real charm. I sometimes wonder if the red Graves do not owe their reputation at least in part to these isolated Vayres Graves, far from the proper Graves area. No-one will pretend that they are great and subtle wines, but they are most pleasant to drink and not too expensive to buy.

BURGUNDY

Chablis

The area occupied by the vineyards of Bourgogne lies partly in the *département* of the Yonne, mainly in that of the Côte-d'Or and Saône-et-Loire. In the Yonne there is only one really fine wine, the *Chablis*, whose *A.C.* covers also *Chablis-Grand-Cru*. The flavour of Chablis is quite its own, for the vineyards are far removed from the heart of Burgundy. They are nearly 90 miles from Dijon, 12 miles east of Auxerre – and Auxerre itself is under 110 miles from Paris. The white wines are pale yellow in colour with the occasional suggestion of a vague touch of green, they are dry, with a very individual, fresh flavour. They are made exclusively from Beaunois or Pinot Chardonnay grapes and have an alcoholic strength of not less than 10°. When the name "Chablis" is followed by that of a locality (*Bougros, Blanchot, Grenouilles, Les Clos, Preuses, Valmur,* and *Vaudésir*), the minimum strength admitted is stepped up to 11°, and the same is true if the title "Chablis-Grand-Cru" figures on the label. There is an intermediate denomination, *Chablis-Premier-Cru,* for wines with not less than 10.5° alcoholic strength.

There is a separate *A.C.* for *Petit-Chablis,* 9.5° degrees only, but made exclusively from Pinot Chardonnay grapes. It is much sharper than the true Chablis, and usually sold much younger. It is also a very refreshing drink, and a great deal cheaper than its more aristocratic cousins.

Côte-d'Or

This is the *département* of the royal Burgundies, some of which also grow in the Saône-et-Loire, the next *département* southwards, but these are few compared to the long list of incomparable wines which grace the Côte-d'Or. Before studying them it is well to have a look at the generic *appellation* wines.

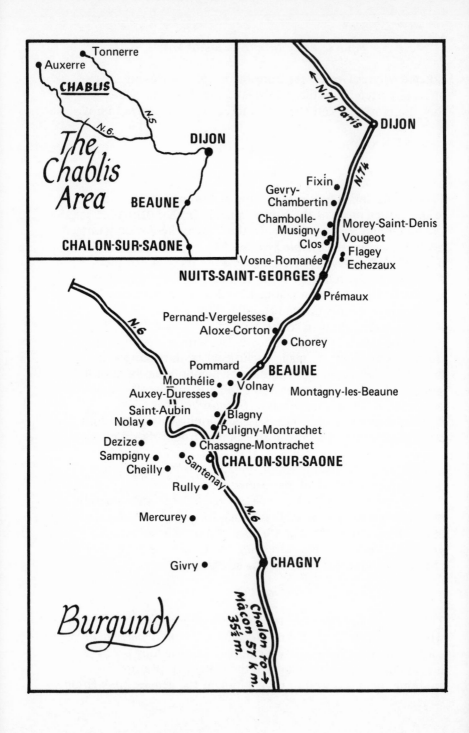

The Chablis Area

Tonnerre
Auxerre
CHABLIS
N.5
N.6.
The Chablis Area
DIJON
BEAUNE
CHALON-SUR-SAONE

N.71 Paris
DIJON
N.74
Fixin
Gevry-Chambertin
Chambolle-Musigny
Morey-Saint-Denis
Vougeot
Clos
Flagey
Vosne-Romanée
Echezaux
NUITS-SAINT-GEORGES
Prémaux
Pernand-Vergelesses
Aloxe-Corton
Chorey
Pommard
BEAUNE
Monthélie
Volnay
Montagny-les-Beaune
Auxey-Duresses
Saint-Aubin
Blagny
Nolay
Puligny-Montrachet
Dezize
Chassagne-Montrachet
Sampigny
Santenay
CHALON-SUR-SAONE
Cheilly
Rully
N.6
Mercurey
Givry
CHAGNY
Burgundy
Chalon to Mâcon 57 k.m. 35½ m.

First is plain *Bourgogne,* covering red, rosé, and white
wines made from grapes grown within the prescribed limits
of the vineyard area of the three *départements.* These grapes
can only be Pinot-blanc or Chardonnay for the white wines,
and Pinot-noirien, Pinot-Liébault, and Pinot-Beurot for the
red and rosé wines. The white wines must reach a minimum
of 10.5^{O} of alcoholic content, the reds 10°. In other words,
plain Bourgogne is a fairly strong wine made from good
grapes grown in good vineyards. In fact it is often better than
its simple title might lead one to believe.

The second *A.C.* covers the curiously named red *Bourgogne-
Passe-Tout-Grains,* which sounds as if anything that might
be called a grape could be accepted for it, but fortunately
this is not true. There is a mixture of grapes at the time of
pressing; at least one-third of them must be Pinot-noirien or
Pinot-Liébault, the rest being Gamay-noir (giving white juice)
and up to 15 per cent of Chardonnay, Pinot-blanc, or Pinot-
gris. A blend of actual wines (such as takes place in Alsace)
is not permitted, even though the various wines were themselves made from the specified grapes. I have met some quite
pleasing examples of this inexpensive wine.

The third generic *appellation* is *Bourgogne-ordinaire,* or
Bourgogne-grand-ordinaire, which means that only Pinot and
Gamay-noir grapes may be used for red and rosé wines. The
choice is made wider for the whites: Pinot-blanc, Chardonnay,
Aligoté, and Melon-de-Bourgogne, a mixture of the good with
the not quite so good. The reds and rosés run only to 9° of
alcohol (against the 10° of the *appellation Bourgogne*) and
the whites 9.5^{O} against 10.5^{O}.

Next is a white wine, *Bourgogne-Aligoté,* made either
exclusively from Aligoté grapes, or from a mixture of Aligoté
and Pinot-Chardonnay. This very dry — almost sharp — wine
goes particularly well with Cassis to make a *vin blanc cassis,*
the inexpensive aperitif already described. I think the universal
use of this 9.5^{O} white wine as an aperitif leads to its being
rather neglected as a table wine. It is a good one with fish or
shellfish.

Now for sparkling wines. Any wine to which the *appellation*
"Bourgogne" can legitimately be applied and which has been
subjected to the double fermentation process (*méthode*

champenoise) can be sold as *Bourgogne-mousseux*. If you demand a sparkling wine that is cheap compared not only with Champagne but with some of the alternatives as well, I suppose there must be some Bourgogne-mousseux which will give you pleasure. In honesty I must say that I have not yet found one which has given me any, but as I have not tried very many since a quite disastrous first experience, you may well put my opinion down to unreasonable prejudice.

Côte-de-Nuits

Between Dijon and Nuits-Saint-Georges is the Côte-de-Nuits, a range of hills studded with vineyards where the grapes are grown which produce some of the world's great wines.

There is a generic *appellation* for the *Vins-fins-de-la-Côte-de-Nuits*. Naturally wines sold under this label are not as fine as those sold under the names of individual vineyards and villages, but they are often very pleasant and never very expensive. They are strong: the reds with 10.5° minimum and the whites with 11°. The reds are made from three excellent Pinot grapes, and the whites from Pinot-blanc and Chardonnay. They therefore have the full Burgundy flavour, but as they are usually sold young, they lack the finesse of older and better ones.

Coming southwards down the N 74 from Dijon the first vineyards are to the west of the main road; none are very far away from it. The very first name to remember is *Fixin (A.C.)* for red and white wines of a high standard. The whites are made only from Pinot-blanc and Chardonnay grapes, the reds from the three classic Burgundy Pinots, Pinot-noirien, Pinot-Beurot, and Pinot-Liébault. From here southwards to the extremes of Burgundy, this choice is universal. This wine is sold normally as having a minimum 10.5° of alcohol, and the *Premier-Cru* 11°.

The wines in this more northern part are on the whole more full-bodied than the more southern ones. They require more time to develop and will age almost indefinitely. When fully developed the experts consider them the finest of all wines; it is true that they become equally splendid in aroma, taste, texture, and colour.

The next centre southwards is *Gevrey-Chambertin (A.C.)*.

The territory of the village of Gevrey included the vineyards
of Chambertin, and when permission was given to the village
in the nineteenth century officially to make its name Gevrey-
Chambertin, *all* wines grown within its area could legitimately
be called by the double-barrelled name. This is a little con-
fusing, for the Chambertin vineyards were not the only ones
within the territory, so that now when you buy a Gevrey-
Chambertin (and a very good wine it is to buy) you do not
necessarily get any Chambertin in it. Shades of Napoleon,
whose favourite wine it was – a rare example of his showing
good taste!

The Chambertins are numerous. They are all rich 11.5°
reds. You can buy *Chambertin, Chambertin-Clos-de-Bèze
(A.C.),* and seven *Premiers-Crus* which are included under
that same *A.C.: Chapelle-Chambertin, Charmes-Chambertin,
Griotte-Chambertin, Latricières-Chambertin, Mazoyères-
Chambertin,* and *Ruchottes-Chambertin.* These are all lovely
wines, and priced according to their quality.

Still going southwards we come next to a cluster of seven
villages, each with an *A.C.* of its own, with individual vineyards overlapping the territories of different villages, which
creates complications. With one exception they are all on
the western side.

First of the cluster is *Morey-Saint-Denis*, making both
reds and whites. The reds are much the same as all the other
good reds in this part of Burgundy, but there is a certain
elegance about the whites which distinguishes them from
others. After the *Clos-de-Tart,* a vineyard with an *A.C.* all of
its own and a great reputation, comes the much smaller
Saint-Denis vineyard, and with it the territorial complications,
for Saint-Denis overlaps the next place down, Bonnes-Mares,
which includes the well-known *Clos-de-la-Roche. Bonnes-
Mares* (an *A.C.*) has a vineyard of the same name, and this
extends into *Chambolle* and a further part of it is in *Morey!*
We need not trouble here with these geographical details
beyond stating them, for what is important is to know the
names of the wines. Their quality is in general very high and
the wines, all reds, are beautifully soft. The vineyards are
often split among a number of part-owners, so that the wines

from them vary a little. For unvarying quality, wines from one-owner vineyard are always to be preferred. *Chambolle-Musigny (A.C.)* makes good wines, but the best come from its *Musigny* vineyard (own *A.C.*). These 11.5⁰ reds are counted among the greatest of the great, "the wines without a flaw", and Heaven forbid they should ever be drunk young. There is also a very beautiful 12⁰ white, which tends to vary from harvest to harvest.

Next southwards comes *Vougeot,* with perhaps the world's most famous vineyard, *Clos-de-Vougeot (A.C.).* The area of the vineyard is somewhat less than 130 acres and it belongs to no fewer than 54 different part-owners. Its interesting old monastic building is the meeting-place for the wine-tastings of the *Chevaliers du Tastevin,* wine-learned gentlemen who dress up in medieval finery to discuss wine – in both senses. There is nothing left unsaid about these red wines, acknowledged throughout the world as being at least the equal of the very best. The Vougeot whites are also delicious, though they are far less well known and do not quite reach the total perfection of the reds.

At this level, on the east side of the road, is the village of *Flagey-Echézaux,* whose vineyards stretch down towards those of Nuits-Saint-Georges. On the other side of the main road are the red wines of *Vosne-Romanée (A.C.)* which have a silken smoothness shared with few others. In addition to the wines bearing this particular *appellation* there are others, including *Romanée-Conti, Richebourg, Romanée,* and *La Tâche,* which are grouped under a separate *appellation* granted to *Romanée-Saint-Vivant:* all are very, very beautiful wines, ranking with the very best.

Now we arrive at *Nuits-Saint-Georges.* This prosperous little town, given over to the wine trade, has its own *A.C.* It is another case of a town or village adding the name of its finest vineyard to its original one: to the original *Nuits* the name of the vineyard of *Saint-Georges* has been added, but the bulk of the wines sold as *Nuits-Saint-Georges* have no connection with that particular vineyard. All the wines, however, are of good body and flavour and, although not comparing with the master-wines already mentioned, make good, honest drinking. They are 10.5⁰ in the red, 11⁰ in the white version, but those sold as *Premier-Cru* are rated 11° and 11.5° respectively.

Côte-de-Beaune

As the Côte-de-Nuits is left behind, we meet another generic *A.C.* covering some very good wines, *Côte-de-Beaune:* the standard red wines have a 10.5° alcohol content, and the whites 11°, with these figures being raised to 11° and 11.5° respectively for those marked *Premier-Cru.* As we come to deal with individual wines, those covered only by the generic *A.C.* will not be marked, but the initials *(A.C.)* will indicate that a wine has a specific *appellation contrôlée* of its own.

The vineyards of *Aloxe-Corton (A.C.)* include some very famous ones producing very high-grade wines, with good whites as well as reds. Probably the very best wines of this Côte, more full-bodied than the others and of outstanding reputation for bouquet and flavour, are *Pernand-Vergelesses (A.C.), Corton (A.C.)* which is linked with *Corton-Charlemagne,* and *Charlemagne* itself. The Emperor Charlemagne, according to some rather doubtful records, helped to found the wine industry of this area. Wines from individual vineyards not quite fulfilling the very stringent conditions limiting the use of these names can be sold as *Aloxe-Corton-Premier-Cru,* which for those of limited means can be an excellent purchase.

Savigny-les-Beaune and *Chorey-les-Beaune* are next south-wards, the former to the west and the latter to the east of the main road – sound red wines which need a long time to mature before reaching their best. And then we come to Beaune itself, that charming town redolent of the product to which it gives its name. It has its own generic *appellation contrôlée,* plain *Beaune,* with the same alcohol content as those of the Côte-de-Nuits, again with stronger wines being sold as *Premier-Cru.* I have personally found the wines of the generic *A.C.* to maintain a very good standard: they are far from being the equal of the great ones, but they make for very enjoyable drinking.

The next of these great wines to be met is *Pommard (A.C.),* a powerful red wine which is a little hard if not kept in bottle for a number of years, after which it becomes vastly improved and a very noble wine. Then, by way of contrast, though only a little way south, we meet the wines of *Volnay (A.C.)*, lighter in body, lighter in colour, more delicate in bouquet.

Still moving south, we reach *Monthélie* and *Auxey-Duresses*, both good but smaller wines coming under the Côte-de-Beaune *A.C.* After them there is another very famous name, *Meursault*, whose own *appellation* covers *Meursault-Côte-de-Beaune* and *Meursault-Blagny* as well, Blagny being the next little village to the south. The white wines are the famous ones. They have a very pleasing bouquet and flavour, and are a little lighter than the white wines from farther north. The reds are good, but not so highly considered as the whites.

It seems that the red and white wines of *Saint-Aubin*, which come under the Côte-de-Beaune *A.C.*, are very little known outside Burgundy itself, which is a pity for they remind one of and are much cheaper than their more favoured neighbours. Very favoured indeed is Saint-Aubin's nearest neighbour southwards, Montrachet.

Montrachet A.C. wines, all whites, are utterly magnificent, subtle in flavour, smooth yet of good body, delightful in colour, agreeable of bouquet. The experts will maintain that only those entitled to be known as *Montrachet* by itself are really supreme. The less expert will be thoroughly content with those that take another name as well, particularly the two with a place name rather than a vineyard name added: *Puligny-Montrachet* more to the north, *Chassagne-Montrachet* to the south and west. The vineyard names are here given in alphabetical order, as it is just not possible to differentiate between them in words: *Bâtard-Montrachet, Bienvenues-Bâtard-Montrachet, Chevalier-Montrachet,* and *Criots-Bâtard-Montrachet.* How happy could one be with a bottle of any one of them!

Before leaving the Côte-de-Beaune there is one important breakdown of the generic *appellation* that must be described, for under the description *Côte-de-Beaune-Villages* there are a number of good and inexpensive wines. The wines sold under this description are blends of two or more of the following: *Côte-de-Beaune, Auxey-Duresses, Blagny, Chassagne-Montrachet, Cheilly-les-Maranges, Chorey, Dezize-les-Maranges, Ladoix, Meursault, Meursault-Blagny, Monthélie, Pernand-*

Vergelesses, Puligny-Montrachet, Saint-Aubin, Sampigny-les-Maranges, Santenay, Savigny.

Saône-et-Loire

It is good-bye to the Côte-de-Beaune, but there are some wines beyond it which, by their quality, still belong to it, as already mentioned. The agreeable reds of *Santenay* still come under the same *appellation.* The reds and whites of *Rully (A.C.)* and the excellent wines of *Mercurey (A.C.),* whites and reds, lead us to big, busy, bustling Mâcon and its *Mâcon* and *Mâcon-supérieur A.C.,* where Burgundy really comes to an end.

Indeed, *Mâcon, Pinot-Chardonnay-Mâcon,* and *Mâcon-Villages* are much more akin to Beaujolais than to Bourgogne and are a long way off the Côte-de-Nuits and the Côte-de-Beaune which this chapter was really about.

Index of Wines

A. C. – *appellation contrôlée*
V. D. Q. S. – *vin délimité de qualité supérieure*
V. P. – *vin de pays*